BISTRO

BISTRO

Trade Secrets from a Life in Food

ALVIN AND GLENNA REBICK

Foreword by Anne Hardy, Editor, *Where to Eat in Canada*

MACMILLAN CANADA
Toronto

First published in Canada in 2000 by
Macmillan Canada, an imprint of CDG Books Canada

Canadian Cataloguing in Publication Data
Rebick, Alvin
Bistro : trade secrets from a life in food
Includes index.

ISBN 0-7715-7697-8
1. Cookery. 2. Restaurants - Anecdotes. I. Rebick, Glenna. II. Title.
TX714.R417 2000   641.5   C00-931273-0

This book is available at special discounts for bulk purchases by your group or organization for sales promotions, premiums, fundraising and seminars. For details, contact: CDG Books Canada Inc., 99 Yorkville Avenue, Suite 400, Toronto, ON, M5R 3K5.

1 2 3 4 5 TRANS-B-G 04 03 02 01 00

Cover and text design by Tania Craan
Illustrations by Glenna Rebick

Macmillan Canada
An imprint of CDG Books Canada Inc.
Toronto

Printed in Canada

To Kael and Terra, our daughters and our best friends

CONTENTS

Foreword

I first ran into Alvin and Glenna Rebick at the Baker Street Bistro in Guelph. At the time, I knew nothing whatever of the problems—the plumbing especially—of running a restaurant in their picturesque old yellow-brick house on Baker Street. I just thought what a neat place it was—not your common or garden storefront eatery, not a hotel with a room for ladies and escorts, but a real little restaurant, like something you might find in Burgundy, with candles and white tablecloths and a modish menu offering things like chicken Mexican-style, Indonesian satays, and sweet-and-sour pork. The soundtrack was cool, and the art exploded off the walls—magic realism in one room, art deco in the other.

By 1987, when I next encountered the Rebicks, restaurants had become the in place to be. Every newspaper had its restaurant columnist, and everyone had a favourite chef. By then, Alvin and Glenna Rebick had just finished nine successful years at the Baker Street Bistro, where they had introduced modern American cooking, then largely unknown in this country, to a small town 60 miles west of Toronto. With their friends Mark and Chris Grenville, they had moved to Ottawa, where there was still little to be had but traditional French, popular Italian, and run-of-the-mill Far Eastern. They settled on Somerset Street and called their restaurant Grenville's. They had an imaginative menu, but imagination is a poor substitute for a thick bankroll. Ottawa people still expected a restaurant to look like a gentleman's club and Grenville's didn't. It was all purple and pink, and the downstairs bar had to be seen to be believed. They weren't the only trendy place on the block, but none of their neighbours had any money either, and before long Grenville's found itself swimming upstream. There were days I was the only person served. As often as not, I'd arrive five minutes before closing time, perhaps with a bunch of people from the office, perhaps with some of my grandchildren. Alvin had kept his standards high and his prices low. He'd make me welcome and set up a table for me, being careful to remember the kids' names and what they liked to eat. There was a lot of good talk. Alvin was comfortably left wing. He liked America—he was American—and he didn't like Ottawa.

I remembered what it had been like to be poor in America, making my way through Penn Station eight months pregnant with a heavy suitcase in one hand and a howling baby in the other. I was one of those people who let the system down, and nobody offered me a hand. So I didn't agree with Alvin about America, or about Ottawa either. But I liked his sesame chicken with its sauce of lemon, parsley, and ketjab manis. I liked his pork tenderloin stuffed with goat cheese and finished with mango, jalapeño, and rum. And I liked his fish, which was beautifully fresh and lightly cooked at a time when fish was overcooked as a matter of course. My four-year-old granddaughter, who was planning to become a waitress, would appear, pencil and paper in hand, to ask each of us if we would have the fish or the sesame chicken. That sesame chicken became famous.

Of course, there was more to Grenville's than sesame chicken. The cooking became more and more exacting and meticulous. At one point, Alvin and Glenna were doing an appetizer sampler for two with up to 16 tiny hors d'oeuvres arranged on a plate with the precision of a Swiss watchmaker. Glenna made some intriguing soups, and Chris Grenville turned out some irresistible chocolate pâtés, just touched with Cointreau and crème anglaise.

After seven years on this beat, they returned to Guelph in 1993 and went to work at the Paramount Café in the Carden Place Hotel. I followed them there, and I well remember a dish of Thai noodles I had before they moved to The Bookshelf Café. It came with shrimp, tofu, bean sprouts, and peanuts for $8.50. With a bottle of wine, served at cost plus $7.00, it was unforgettable.

For years now they have been wedged between bookshelves and kitchen, doing what they do best with a minimum of fuss and little or no space. But this year, the Bookshelf has taken over and renovated the building next door and soon the Rebicks will have, for the first time since they left Ottawa, room to move and room to breathe. Even with the new space and its demands, hopefully Glenna will still find time for her painting and Alvin for his garden. And together they will think up new ways to serve sesame chicken.

Anne Hardy
Ottawa, March 2000

Introduction

As I sit at my desk, Glenna working close by, editing the recipes that we have been compiling for the past two months, I find myself pleasantly surprised by how enjoyable this process has been. Looking back at 22 years spent working side by side in the restaurant industry might have caused anxiety. After all, we are past 50, still doing much the same work we did before turning 30 and are likely to be doing so for some time to come. Glenna still stands behind the stoves and pumps out the food while I wait on tables. The jobs haven't gotten any easier and the remuneration continues a long decline. Facing these realities by writing a cooking memoir together has been energizing rather than depressing, though you might not notice that by looking at me.

It never ceases to amaze me how simpatico Glenna and I are when it comes to getting a job done. An independent project, such as this one, confirms how supportive and cooperative we are. We recognized early in our relationship that we didn't annoy each other. It was easy and comfortable for us to be together and unlike in the business world, none of the small stuff gets in the way. We are a democracy of two and working together on a personal project has always been particularly rewarding. I am certain that this is partly the reason our children have grown up to be such splendidly individual young women. It certainly couldn't have been easy for them, having parents whose work kept them out of the house much of the time and exhausted most of the rest. Of course, there are advantages to being young adolescents with trusting parents who are rather eccentric and rarely home. Better to experiment in your own house than out on the street.

Another integral ingredient in our lives together is the food we make. Not long ago, the marketing committee at The Bookshelf cornered me and asked for some copy to describe the new menu we were preparing for a six-figure restaurant renovation nearing completion. As always, I had very little to contribute. "Well, it's not Chinese!" I said. They weren't amused. I wasn't trying to be sarcastic, it's just difficult to put into words a cuisine that is the fusion of 20 years' work. The words I would choose are simple, fresh, and flavourful. Hardly language that would make for a successful ad campaign.

Though responsive to the environment in which it is being presented, the food Glenna and I prepare is always of a certain character. Neither of us likes salt or pretension. Dining at Grenville's in the spring of 1988, Robert Sidi, a noted Toronto restauranteur, commented that our food was very honest. I couldn't have said it better myself.

And yes, we have just opened a new restaurant! I have heard that women forget the pain of childbirth, no matter how severe, when graced with the joy of a newborn. I wish the same could be said for birthing a bistro! We just became proud parents of yet another establishment as The Bookshelf Café has been reborn once again. And how very beautiful and very exhausting it is. Thank goodness we have had the opportunity to reflect on our history, compile the best of what we have created, and take energy from what we've accomplished. We're going to need it!

Art and Onions

Traditionally, in the family home, the woman is the cook. Both my mother, Lil, and Alvin's mother, Ruth, have admitted that they never really enjoyed cooking. It was a chore, their duty, something required of them, as they had a family to feed. Each developed favourites; Lil's dills, homemade mustards, and Romanian eggplant salad, or Ruth's potato and noodle "kugel" and sweet-and-sour cabbage soup.

For me, cooking, and all things domestic, are shared responsibilities. Cooking is also my livelihood. Surprisingly, making a meal at home is rarely a chore but rather easy, relaxing, and comfortable.

I can't remember who said it, but I'll never forget hearing the words, "God forbid you should come into my house and not find a red onion!" My sentiments exactly!

Onions appear in every cuisine, cross all cultures and generations, and grow under almost any condition. For me, they are a basic ingredient to almost everything I create in the kitchen. Like the underpainting behind a finished canvas, the onions are the foundation of a recipe. Mix them with garlic and butter or olive oil to start building a soup, a relish or a stew. Like the primary colours, red, blue, and yellow, onions are the essence of cooking.

Much depends on how you slice them, or dice them, chop, julienne, or mince them. You can roast, grill, sweat, steam, simmer, and stew them or watch them brown or turn transparent. Caramelized, marinated, tossed, blended, whisked or puréed, sautéed, or stirred constantly, the result changes with the technique.

It's also in the variety ... red, green, white, Vidalia or Walla-Walla, leek, shallot, chive, and pearl. Water colour, acrylic or oil, brush stroke, staining, scraping, or layering, it all comes down to art and onions for me.

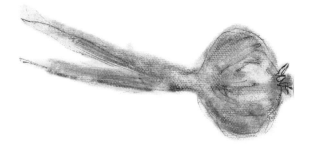

The Bistro Pantry

Not coincidentally, people who have visited our home and feel close enough to us to speak their minds, consistently complain about the same two things. One is that it's never warm enough in winter and the other is the lack of anything to munch. We have responded to the "I'm freezing!" complaint by having an enormous collection of throws and afghans that are within reach of every relaxing chair. The remarks about food are ignored.

This is not to say that visitors aren't satisfied at meal times. It's just that if you were to open our refrigerator, there might be little more than a bottle of wine, some olives, and a few condiments. Having been in the restaurant business for most of our adult lives, we don't see food purchasing in the same way as the average householder does. A week's worth of groceries makes little sense in the grand scheme of things when products like lemons, lettuce, and lamb chops come by the case, not the pound, and food cost is something that is figured in percentages rather than grocery receipts. For the same reason, we grow flowers, not vegetables, because we could never compete with the bounty of produce that appears in our professional kitchen daily, as if by magic.

Then how do we manage to create meals at home with so few raw materials? By stocking the pantry with items that, when you add the fresh ingredients, bring a meal to life. This wasn't much comfort to our girls when they came home from school with hungry friends and had little more to offer than some Carr's Water Biscuits, a red onion, and some feta cheese. "Wait until Alvin or Glenna gets home, they'll feed us!" they would say. They knew, no matter how slim the pickings, their parents would always prepare something great to eat.

The items that make up a Bistro Pantry are not for immediate gratification. You have to combine them with fresh ingredients in order to create something worth waiting for. If a dish needs inspiration, the long list of items that follow will work to enliven even the most ordinary food.

THINGS THAT COME IN CANS

- black beans
- chickpeas
- coconut milk
- diced tomatoes
- kidney beans
- tomato juice
- tomato paste
- tuna
- whole tomatoes

THINGS THAT COME IN BAGS

- almonds, sliced or slivered
- basmati rice
- coarse salt
- cornmeal
- currants
- pasta, all different kinds
- peanuts
- pecans
- raisins
- rice noodles
- rolled oats
- sesame seeds
- sun-dried tomatoes
- white rice

THINGS THAT COME IN JARS

- anchovies
- Asian chili sauce, hot
- capers
- chili paste
- chili sauce, sweet
- chutney
- good quality relish
- hot peppers
- ketchup
- ketjab manis (Indonesian soy sauce)
- maple syrup
- marmalade
- mayonnaise
- mustard—Dijon, honey, grain
- oils—olive, extra-virgin olive, canola, sesame
- olives
- peanut butter
- salsa
- soy sauce
- Tabasco
- vinegar—white, wine, aged balsamic, rice
- Worcestershire sauce

ESSENTIAL DRIED HERBS AND SPICES

- basil
- cayenne
- chili peppers
- chili powder
- cinnamon
- cloves
- coriander
- cumin
- curry powder
- dry mustard
- garlic powder
- nutmeg
- oregano
- paprika
- peppercorns
- rosemary
- tarragon
- thyme
- turmeric
- white pepper

Tips from the Trenches

- Use almost-empty jars of mayonnaise, mustard, chili sauce, ketchup, and maple syrup as the base for salad dressings. The jar becomes the shaker and container.
- Add chili sauce (hot or sweet) to stews or soups to enliven the flavour.
- Tomato juice added to tomato-based soups and sauces works as a quick solution if more stock or liquid is needed. Used as part of the water portion when cooking rice, tomato juice adds a new dimension.
- Marmalade stirred into curries and Asian-inspired dishes brightens the taste.
- For a hotter "kick" to Mexican and Indian-inspired dishes, add a bit of salsa or chili paste.
- Toasted almonds sprinkled in salads add taste and texture.
- Should unexpected company arrive or if you're at your wits' end about something quick to make for dinner, the sketches that follow will serve you in good stead.

An Instant Soup

1 can chickpeas, 1 can kidney beans, 1 onion, 2 carrots, cumin, and cinnamon for seasoning. Sauté the onions in oil, add julienned carrots, cumin and cinnamon, some salt and pepper and 4 cups of stock or water. Add chickpeas with some of their liquid. Add drained beans and cook until carrots are tender. The addition of 1 bunch of chopped spinach 2 minutes before serving makes a good soup better.

Glazed Chicken or Fish

Combine equal parts of one of the following with mayonnaise:

salsa

chili sauce

chutney

mustard

relish

Spread it atop chicken or firm-fleshed fish and bake for about 30 minutes or until done.

Mexican Beans

Sauté some onions, garlic, and beans, add chili powder, cumin, and chopped pickled jalapeños and mash the beans. Cook a little longer after mashing and combine with some salsa, wrap in flour tortilla, sprinkle with cheese, and bake. Makes a great taco too.

Instant Chinese

Combine some chopped garlic and ginger, soy sauce, marmalade or maple syrup, and orange juice in a bowl and throw in some sliced chicken breasts and/or peeled shrimp to marinate. After 1/2 hour, toss in a wok with any vegetables and the marinade. Serve with basmati rice and top with toasted nuts and chopped green onions.

Simple Baked Fish

Cut up some veggies (onion, carrots, celery, pepper, zucchini, etc.) and place on top of fish fillets (salmon, trout, or halibut) as they sit in a baking dish. Pour 1 cup tomato juice and 1/2 cup white wine over the fish and veg. Sprinkle with salt and pepper, add a splash of Tabasco and Worcestershire sauce, then cover with foil and bake for 30 minutes at 350° F. Serve with rice or mashed potatoes.

SOUP OF THE DAY

From Brooklyn to Pembroke

Split Pea Soup with Ginger

Harvest Vegetable Soup

Three-Mushroom Soup

Black Bean and Corn Chowder

Tortilla Tomato Soup

Tomato Cream Cheese Soup

Curried Lentil and Sweet Potato Soup

Grandma Ruth's Chicken Soup

Dilled Beet and Potato Soup

Gazpacho

Fruited Gazpacho

From Brooklyn to Pembroke

In my grandmother Bess's dark, cluttered, Brooklyn kitchen, there was always a large, copper-bottomed, stainless steel pot, bubbling loudly on the gas burner. The kitchen was humid with the soup. My grandmother sat in a wheelchair, her hair in a wispy chignon, eyes sparkling like currants set in soft clouds. Grandma was at the counter, making dough from matzo meal for the knadlach that would float like golf balls in her chicken soup. She smiled when she saw me enter the room and grabbed at me as I slipped past, trying to avoid a loving pinch from her sticky fingers. She questioned me in a Yiddish that is now only a vague memory. I told her that I wanted to look at the soup and dragged over the shaky, metal stepladder. She wheeled over and quickly turned down the flame.

Scrambling up the two steps, I cautiously tilted my head into the misty void. I looked in through the steam that took my breath away and saw a slick, greenish reflecting pool. Floating below were chunks of carrot, familiar and vaguely pretty. Suddenly, bubbling up from the depths, appeared a gaping, bony neck and three horrible clawed feet covered in a milky yellow skin. Terrified, I pulled back, almost falling off the ladder, and fled from the room, vowing never to eat soup again.

Fast-forward 20 years, and I am as far removed from that kitchen in Brooklyn as it is possible to imagine. I live on a homestead in the Ottawa Valley with a gaggle of friends, my wife Glenna, and our beautiful, eighteen-month-old daughter, Kael. The farm, Spring Green, sits on 160 acres of sparse, rocky field mixed with young hardwood brush. A narrow, tree-lined drive leads to a huge, aluminum-clad house and a tumble-down barnyard surrounded by a selection of tired, slanting buildings in various stages of disrepair. The most architecturally significant is a century-old log chicken coop, wherein live 12 white, leghorn chickens. There is not a Jewish grandmother within a hundred miles, so I am safe from the soup.

It's not that soup isn't an integral part of my eating life. The crew that lives at Spring Green, enthusiastic vegetarians all, are very fond of soup. As well, we bake bread in an old wood stove named Roy, pump water from the well outside the summer kitchen door, bathe at night by the glow of kerosene lamps and believe that we can change the world by turning our backs on it. We grow half an acre of potatoes, squashing by hand the crunchy, brown beetles that would settle for an early harvest. In addition, we bake muffins to sell at the local market (though here in Pembroke, we are so exotic that none but the bravest will buy our wares), and keep chickens for the eggs.

Since moving to Spring Green, I've discovered that chicken soup is not my only fear. The summer bathing ritual keeps me awake at night. When the weather turns warm, we move outside to the well where, stark naked, one stands with soap and a washcloth, lathering all over, while a friend pumps freezing water into a worn, wooden pail. When the bather is ready, the sadist gleefully hurls the water to shrieks of pain and exhilaration. When it is my turn, I run soapy and humiliated from the yard, unable to bear the thought of the icy water. My pursuer chases me down the path that leads past the kitchen garden towards the algae-covered pond. I jump into the disgusting, slimy, green pool, my feet sinking into the soft, sucking bottom that, though revolting, is better than the freezing water. Everyone has assembled to laugh at the antics, but I refuse to emerge until all have departed. There are no chicken parts anywhere to be seen, though the water has an eerie, green familiarity.

Every morning and evening, it is someone's chore to enter the henhouse and retrieve warm eggs from under the clucking, fat bodies of its residents. City kids all, we love the idea of chores and work hard at tasks that our suburban parents shake their groomed heads over. They wonder how we can take such pleasure in pumping water, filling lamps, splitting wood to feed the hungry furnace, or wrestling crabgrass out of hardscrabble soil. We are smugly disdainful.

One fateful morning, it is my turn to gather the eggs and so, placing Kael on my hip, I saunter to the henhouse. I stoop to avoid the lintel and enter the dimly lit enclave. I move to put Kael down, but she clamps her legs tightly around me as a warning of her desire to remain lifted. The chickens talk their talk, an odd mix of cooing and threat. I like to feel in control, as if born to do this, but as always around animals, I'm a touch wary. In my eagerness to do the job right, I have foolishly left the door to the barnyard open. Like the caged animals they are, sensing the opportunity for flight, the 12 leghorns simultaneously rush for the door and escape into the daylight. Awkwardly clutching my daughter, I charge out into the yard and try to deal with the pandemonium. A fellow farm dweller with more experience yells, "By the feet! Grab them by the feet!" With my one free hand, I lunge for the closest escapee and grab for the aforementioned appendage. Seeing the wrinkled feet, bright red as they are, brings on an immediate flashback to my grandmother's kitchen and its bubbling soup pot. I scream, drop Kael, and run for the hills.

There are no hills and, being a devoted father, I quickly get control of myself, rush back and scoop up the shrieking, abandoned child and flee the yard as quickly as my feet can carry me. Needless to say, I tragically transmitted my fear of chicken feet to my unsuspecting child. Although reconciled to soup, we have both been known to scurry past chicken-hung windows in Chinatown rather than have our eyes fall on those dangling limbs. I suppose it could be worse; she could be afraid of her grandmother.

Split Pea Soup with Ginger

SERVES 6

2 cups green or yellow split peas, rinsed

1-inch piece fresh ginger, peeled
and minced

2 cloves garlic, minced

3 stalks celery, chopped

1 large onion, chopped

1 large carrot, sliced

1 Tbsp. unsalted butter or olive oil

4-6 cups water or chicken stock

salt and ground pepper, to taste

splash of maple syrup

METHOD

In a large soup pot, place the peas and cover with water until half the pot is filled. Bring to a boil, lower temperature to medium high and cook for about 20 minutes. Foam will appear on the top of the water and should be skimmed off with a spoon.

Meanwhile, sauté ginger, garlic and vegetables in the butter or oil until vegetables are soft. Add vegetables to simmering peas along with water or chicken stock and continue cooking for 1 to 2 hours until peas are completely soft, stirring occasionally. Season generously with salt and pepper and stir in maple syrup. Add more water or stock if soup is too thick.

For a thick, smooth texture, purée in a food processor or with a hand blender.

Harvest Vegetable Soup

SERVES 6-8

2 cloves garlic, minced

1 large onion, chopped

3 stalks celery, sliced

1 Tbsp. unsalted butter

4 potatoes, peeled and coarsely chopped

2 sweet potatoes, peeled and coarsely chopped

1 small squash, peeled and coarsely chopped

1 small turnip, peeled and chopped

2 large carrots, peeled and sliced

1 parsnip, peeled and sliced (optional)

1 tsp. cumin

1 tsp. chili powder

1/2 tsp. curry powder

salt and ground pepper, to taste

vegetable stock, chicken stock, or water

1 cup whipping cream (optional)

METHOD

In a large pot, sauté garlic, onions, and celery in the butter until onions are soft. Add the rest of the vegetables with the spices, stirring to combine. Pour in stock or water to generously cover vegetables, bring to a boil, lower heat, and continue cooking until the veggies are soft, about 1 hour. Don't hesitate to add more liquid if you think it is necessary. Remove from heat and purée using food processor or hand blender. If the soup is too thick, add more liquid. If you want a richer soup, add a cup of whipping cream. This soup feeds a crowd, tastes better the next day, and freezes well for later use.

Using the same vegetables, you can create a different soup by changing the spicing. Try parsley, white pepper, thyme, and a pinch of nutmeg.

Three-Mushroom Soup

1 large onion, diced

2 cloves garlic, minced

3 Tbsp. unsalted butter

6 cups white mushrooms, sliced

3 cups oyster mushrooms, sliced

1 large portobello mushroom, halved
   and sliced

1 heaping tsp. Dijon mustard

1 Tbsp. tarragon leaves

1 tsp. thyme leaves

pinch of white pepper

splash of Worcestershire sauce

1 tsp. salt

ground black pepper, to taste

3 Tbsp. all-purpose flour

4 cups chicken or vegetable stock

1 cup milk

1/4 cup dry sherry

METHOD

In a large soup pot, sauté onions and garlic in butter until onions begin to wilt. Add mushrooms and continue cooking until they begin to brown and give off liquid. Add seasonings and stir. Sprinkle in flour and mix in throughly to make a roux. Slowly add stock, milk, and sherry, stirring to combine and thicken. Simmer, stirring occasionally for about 1 hour. Avoid bringing to full boil. Taste and season accordingly.

Black Bean and Corn Chowder

2 cups black beans, cleaned and soaked overnight

1 large onion, chopped

3 cloves garlic, minced

3 stalks celery, diced

2 carrots, diced

2 Tbsp. olive oil

1 sweet red pepper, seeded and diced

1 Tbsp. oregano

1 Tbsp. cumin

1 Tbsp. chili powder

1/2 tsp. dried coriander

juice of 2 limes

4 cups stock or water

1 cup tomato juice or tomato sauce

salt and ground pepper, to taste

2 cups fresh or frozen corn kernels

1/4 cup coriander leaves, chopped

sour cream (optional)

Monterey Jack cheese (optional)

METHOD

Cook beans in a pot with enough water to generously cover and boil for about 1 hour, removing foam that forms on the top with a spoon. In a separate large soup pot, sauté onions, garlic, celery, carrots, and sweet pepper in olive oil until vegetables begin to soften. Stir in seasonings (except fresh coriander) and lime juice and cook a few minutes longer. Add beans with their liquid, the stock and the tomato juice or sauce and simmer for at least an hour. Add the corn and the fresh coriander and cook until the corn is soft. Taste, adjust seasoning and serve topped with a dollop of sour cream and a bit of grated Monterey Jack cheese.

When cooking beans, a covered pot makes for a creamier texture. If you can't soak beans overnight, an alternative trick is to boil unsoaked beans for 1 minute, let stand for 1 hour, drain and proceed as for soaked beans.

Tortilla Tomato Soup

My daughter Terra is, not surprisingly, a very good cook. Thankfully, she has not chosen the culinary arts as her profession. Her love of food and feeding people, along with her natural cooking ability and great taste, make me worry that one day she will throw off her legal gown and skip merrily into the kitchen, to be lost forever. A proud father's nightmare!

The recipe that follows is almost as easy as opening a can of Campbell's. If you wish to forgo the formality of making your own tomato soup, then, by all means use canned. This is simple good food at its best, just the way Terra likes it!

1 large onion, chopped

2 cloves garlic, minced

1 Tbsp. cumin

pinch of ground coriander

1 Tbsp. chili powder

1 Tbsp. oregano

pinch of cayenne

1 Tbsp. olive oil

1 cup nacho chips, coarsely chopped

1 cup tomato juice or puréed canned tomatoes

1 cup chicken stock or water

salsa, fresh coriander, grated cheese, sour cream to garnish (optional)

METHOD

Sauté onions and garlic with the spices in oil briefly, stir in nacho chips, add tomato juice and stock, and then bring to a boil. Reduce to simmer for 30 minutes, taste and adjust spicing. Garnish with any or all of: salsa, more nacho chips, fresh coriander, grated cheese, or sour cream.

Tomato Cream Cheese Soup

Neither the staff nor the public were particularly thrilled when Glenna and I became managers at The Bookshelf Café. Business had been declining for years, and from what I observed both in the dining room and on the plate, emergency action was necessary. Nevertheless, old habits die hard and change, even long overdue, can be met with great resistance.

For some reason, the existing staff thought that I was some sort of ogre who was going to be hell to work for. One woman, a friend of the owners who had a son working at the bar, called and warned them that I was too much of an autocrat to work at such a cooperative venture. Hogwash! This person had never entered any of my restaurants, let alone seen how I operate. It was just the buzz generated by what was seen as a hostile takeover.

The change that brought the biggest hue and cry from the public was the elimination from the menu of Tomato Cream Cheese Soup. I, for one, believe that making a new soup daily is the way a kitchen should function, and I don't consider any recipe worthy of a permanent menu position. I was also appalled when I saw the huge hunks of white cheese floating in the soup pot the first

day I entered the kitchen. Therefore, I banished the soup and was the object of public derision for months.

Little by little I succumbed to pressure. This soup is allowed to be made once in a while, when something speedy is required. It never fails that people will look up from their bowls and tell me, every time, that it is the best soup they have ever tasted. Luckily, I'm not afraid to admit when I'm wrong!

SERVES 6

3 large onions, chopped

3 sprigs dill, chopped

2 Tbsp. vegetable oil

2 28 oz. cans crushed tomatoes

salt and ground pepper, to taste

1 cup cream cheese, cut in small pieces

METHOD

In a soup pot, sauté onions and dill in the oil until softened. Add the canned tomatoes, salt, and a generous amount of pepper. Bring to a boil. Drop in the cream cheese and cook for 1/2 hour. Taste and add more salt and pepper if necessary. Add water to thin if soup is too thick.

Curried Lentil and Sweet Potato Soup

SERVES 6

2 cups dried red lentils, rinsed

1 onion, diced

2 cloves garlic, minced

1-inch fresh ginger, peeled and
   finely chopped

1 Tbsp. unsalted butter or oil

splash of white wine

1 large carrot, chopped

1 stalk celery, sliced

2 sweet potatoes, peeled and diced

1 Tbsp. curry powder

1 tsp. ground cardamom

1 tsp. ground cumin

8 cups stock or water

1 Tbsp. orange marmalade

1 tsp. salt

ground black pepper, to taste

fresh coriander

yogourt

METHOD

In a large soup pot, cook the lentils in enough water to cover generously and skim the foam that forms on top. Meanwhile, in another pot, sauté the onions, garlic, and ginger in the butter or oil until onions turn transparent. Deglaze with a splash of white wine, then add carrots, celery, sweet potatoes, and spices and continue cooking. Transfer the vegetables to the lentil pot and add water or stock. Add marmalade, salt, and ground pepper and simmer until lentils are soft, approximately 1 hour. Taste and season accordingly. Garnish with fresh coriander and a dollop of plain yogourt.

Grandma Ruth's Chicken Soup

My father died recently, after a long illness, and my mother has come to live with Glenna and me. Ruth, like her mother Bess before her, has always made the most delicious chicken soup. One of the many reasons we feel blessed to have her with us is the time she has to teach us some treasured recipes of the past. Out of kindness to me, she has omitted the chicken feet.

SERVES 6-8

1 large carrot, cut in three

1 stalk celery

1 large onion, quartered

2 sprigs fresh dill

2 whole chicken breasts

2 chicken thighs

16 cups water

salt and pepper, to taste

METHOD

In a food processor or blender, finely chop the vegetables and dill. In a large soup pot, place the chicken in water with the finely chopped vegetables, dill, and salt and pepper. Bring to a boil and simmer, covered, for 1 to 2 hours until chicken is cooked. Remove the chicken.

The cooked chicken can be chopped and added to the soup for a heartier meal. It can be used to make your favourite chicken salad, as a filling for enchiladas or crepes, or tossed with sauce for pasta.

Any leftover soup can be frozen and used as chicken stock.

Dilled Beet and Potato Soup

SERVES 4-6

4 medium-size beets, washed

2 Tbsp. unsalted butter

1 large onion, chopped

1/4 cup fresh dill, chopped

4 medium potatoes, peeled and
   coarsely chopped

8 cups water or vegetable stock

salt and pepper, to taste

METHOD

Place beets, with skins still on, in a pot with water to cover, and bring to a boil. Allow to cook until soft enough to pierce with a fork, then remove from heat, drain, and set aside.

Meanwhile, in a large soup pot, melt the butter and sauté the onion with the dill, until the onions are translucent. Add the potatoes and continue to cook for a few minutes longer so that the flavours mingle. Add 8 cups vegetable stock or water and bring to a boil. When the beets have cooled, peel and coarsely chop and add to the soup pot. Continue cooking for approximately 1/2 hour and then purée with a food processor or hand blender. Add salt and pepper to taste. The soup should be thick, smooth, and an absolutely glorious colour.

Do not cook the soup for too long or the beets will lose their colour. If butterfat is not a concern to you, add a cup of whipping cream when you purée the soup or serve with a generous dollop of sour cream and watch the colour change to a beautiful magenta. Delicious hot or cold!

Gazpacho

SERVES 4-6

1 English cucumber

1 red or yellow pepper, or both, seeded

1 green pepper, seeded

1 red onion

4 ripe tomatoes, cored

1 jalapeño pepper, seeded (optional)

1 clove garlic, minced

4 cups tomato juice

splash of red wine or balsamic vinegar

salt and ground pepper (optional)

METHOD

In a food processor, or by hand, chop vegetables and transfer to a large bowl. Vegetables can be course or fine, depending on your preference. Stir in tomato juice and season with salt and ground pepper. Optional additions include chopped fresh basil, dill, or parsley. If you want the soup to be spicy, you can add two tablespoons of salsa for a bit of a kick. Chill and serve with some chopped cucumber, herbed croutons, or fresh herb as a garnish.

Fruited Gazpacho

SERVES 4-6

Chilled soups are often sweet enough to be served for dessert.

1/2 cantaloupe, seeded

1 mango, peeled and pitted

3 peaches, peeled and pitted

1 cup strawberries (optional),
  stems removed

1/4 watermelon, seeded

1/2 English cucumber

1 small red onion

1 cup orange juice

2 cups plain yogourt

pinch of salt

fresh mint

METHOD

Finely chop vegetables and fruit in a food processor or by hand and place in large bowl. Add orange juice, yogourt, salt, and some chopped mint. Stir all ingredients and chill. Be sure to stir again before serving. Garnish with fresh mint leaves.

You may substitute any summer fruit for those suggested in this recipe. Process further to make a delicious smoothie, omitting onion and cucumber, and enjoy any time of day.

STARTERS & SALADS

The Bistro

STARTERS

Spicy Skewered Shrimp

Chicken Sesame Tenderloins with Indonesian
   Dipping Sauce

Spring Rolls

Eggplant Stuffed with Spinach and Goat Cheese

Ahmed's Thai Mussels

Crostini with Oyster Mushrooms and Asiago Cheese

Quesadillas—Two Ways

Tomato Bruschetta

SALADS

Greek Stuffed Summer Tomatoes

Avocado, Endive, and Grapefruit with Citrus Honey
   Mustard Vinaigrette

Cleopatra Salad

Cobb Salad with Ranch Dressing

Laura's Holiday Salad

The Bistro

The Baker Street Bistro began life in 1977 as a cozy, 20-seat dining room with rust velveteen banquettes, French doors, intimate lighting, stained hardwood flours, and a big, ex-pro-football player named Bill Starr shoehorned into its miniscule galley kitchen.

Like many before him, Bill found the day-to-day grind of running a restaurant to be far more rigorous than he'd imagined. A big city boy, bored in a small Ontario town, he loved creating The Bistro, but quickly realized that the commitment was like having a child that never grows up. One morning, he awoke on the floor of the seedy back storage room where he'd been sleeping since his marriage had gone belly up and realized how fed up he was with "this pencil-necked hick town." He longed to go back to New York, open a bar with his brothers, and try to pick up some acting work playing thugs or cops in TV movies.

Enter Alvin stage right. I had never aspired to owning a restaurant. I just happened to be walking down Baker Street one day and saw a new little café in a rundown yellow brick building. I walked up the stairs to take a peek, and the rest is history.

The fact that Bill and I were both New Yorkers may have had something to do with our instant rapport. Perhaps Bill knew a sucker when he saw one. All I know is, one day we traded keys. He got my 1969 blue Mercedes Benz 220 and I got the Bistro!

The years spent on Baker Street were full of hard work, success, frustration, and fun. I have stared blankly at people who insist that they remember wonderful "Bistro" moments that are nowhere in my memory. I suppose that when a restaurant has been a success, it has an energy of its own, and patrons, as well as the proprietor, can stake a claim to their own reality. Forgive me if I don't remember the night you got engaged and danced cheek-to-cheek to a Jobim song. It was probably the same night that the bathtub upstairs overflowed into the kitchen while I was cooking to a full house, blowing the lights, and dumping buckets of water on my head. And who could forget the cockroaches?

Since the place has been closed for years, I can admit without hesitation, that it was crawling with those invasive little creatures with the crunchy bodies and long antennae. 76A Baker Street was an old, decrepit building with a miserable, tightwad landlord, and no matter how hard we scrubbed, sprayed, screamed, or stomped, the bugs prevailed. This was no greasy spoon I'm talking about. We ran a fine-dining establishment with a first-class reputation and a booming business, but there were evenings when I scooped a marching critter right off the table while waxing profoundly about the evening's specials.

One night, when Glenna was pouring wine from a beautiful ceramic carafe, a baby cockroach plopped right into the glass. With great reflexes and class, she swiftly removed everything, saying simply, "oops ... cork!"

I remember waking from a terrifying dream of huge quivering antennae emerging from behind the splintering banquettes as a giant cockroach began to steadily march up the walls. I jumped out of bed, phoned Willie, my real estate agent, and put the business up for sale.

STARTERS

Spicy Skewered Shrimp

The process of marinating, basting, and grilling makes for succulent and delicious shrimp. You can use metal or wooden skewers.

SERVES 4-6

Marinade for 1 lb. large shrimp:

1/2 tsp. salt

1/4 tsp. granulated sugar

pinch of cayenne pepper

1 Tbsp. vermouth or dry sherry

1 Tbsp. sesame oil

2 cloves garlic, minced

1 Tbsp. lemon juice

Combine ingredients, toss with 1 pound peeled and deveined large shrimp and let sit for at least 30 minutes.

GRILLING SAUCE

Combine:

3 Tbsp. ketchup

1 Tbsp. vermouth or dry sherry

1 Tbsp. water

1 Tbsp. Worcestershire sauce

1 Tbsp. chili paste

1 tsp. sesame oil

METHOD

Soak wooden skewers in water for at least 10 minutes. Thread skewer through both ends of each shrimp until there are at least 4 or 5 shrimp on each. Baste with grilling sauce using a pastry brush. Place on lightly oiled hot grill or barbecue, or under the broiler, and quickly turn skewers. Baste again and remove from heat when shrimp have turned pink and firm. Do not overcook! Baste again and serve on chiffonade of lettuce with a wedge of lemon per serving.

For a lovely garnish, slice half an English cucumber very thin. Place in a small bowl and season with coarse salt, pepper, a pinch of granulated sugar, and a splash of white or rice vinegar. Stir and let sit about 30 minutes before serving.

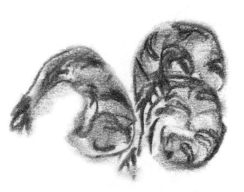

Chicken Sesame Tenderloins with Indonesian Dipping Sauce

We have been making Chicken Sesame in one form or another for many years. No matter how we present this chicken, it is a sensation. I have often said, facetiously, that we could rival McDonald's for the number of Chicken Sesames we have served. Perhaps the best thing about this dish is that it pleases absolutely every taste. Even fussy eaters will love the crispy crust, moist chicken, and smooth, smoky sauce.

SERVES 4 APPETIZER PORTIONS

1 lb. chicken tenderloins

2 eggs, beaten with a splash of water or milk

1 cup all-purpose flour

3/4 cup breadcrumbs

1/4 cup sesame seeds

1 Tbsp. grated parmesan

METHOD

Fill three separate shallow dishes with:
    1) the eggs
    2) flour
    3) the breadcrumbs, sesame seeds, and parmesan mixed together

Dredge chicken tenderloins first in the egg mixture, then the flour, coating well, and finally, in the breadcrumb/sesame seed mixture. Traditionally, we shallow fry the chicken in canola oil until golden brown and place on a baking sheet to finish in the oven. If you wish to bake the chicken, set on a baking pan and place in the oven at 350° F for 10 to 15 minutes until golden.

INDONESIAN DIPPING SAUCE

1/3 cup yogourt

1/3 cup sour cream

2 Tbsp. mayonnaise

1 Tbsp. ketjab manis (Indonesian soy sauce)

METHOD

Mix all ingredients together. The sauce will be a brownish shade of beige that would be a nice colour to paint your living room. If you want the sauce to have a stronger flavour, add a bit more ketjab manis.

This can also be a great main course using boneless chicken breast rather than tenderloins. Drizzle with the following sauce: 1 tablespoon melted butter, minced fresh parsley, 1 tablespoon lemon juice and a generous splash of ketjab manis. Accompany with rice and vegetables of choice.

Spring Rolls

Use store-bought spring roll wrappers, which are available at most Asian grocers.

FOR THE FILLING

3 cups napa cabbage, shredded

1 scant tsp. salt

1/4 cup green onions, finely chopped

1/2 cup carrots, grated

1/2 cup peas, fresh or frozen

1 tsp. sesame oil

1 Tbsp. hot chili sauce or spicy tomato salsa

pinch of salt

1 package ready-made spring roll wrappers, either fresh or frozen

canola oil for frying

1 egg, beaten

METHOD

Combine shredded cabbage and salt in a colander and press it down using a heavy plate. Allow cabbage to drain for 30 minutes, squeezing out any excess moisture. Toss with the remaining ingredients (except the wrappers, canola oil, and egg), using tongs.

TO ROLL

Lay an individual spring roll wrapper on a flat surface with one corner facing towards you. Place approximately 1 heaping tablespoon of filling in the centre. Be sure to squeeze the excess moisture out of the filling before placing it on the wrapper. Starting with the corner closest to you, begin rolling the filling into the wrapper, forming a tight little cigar-shaped package. As you are rolling, tuck in the edges so that the package is tight. Use an egg wash (the beaten egg) to seal the edges and corners, pressing firmly with your fingertips. Repeat with fresh wrappers until the filling is all used. Place finished rolls on a sheet of waxed paper until ready to cook, keeping in mind that they will not last long. Should there be any wrappers left, store in plastic wrap and freeze.

To cook spring rolls, deep fry in very hot canola oil until golden. Remove from oil and drain on a paper towel. Serve immediately.

DIPPING SAUCE

1/4 cup granulated sugar

1/3 cup water

2 Tbsp. rice vinegar

2 Tbsp. orange juice

1 Tbsp. soy sauce

1 Tbsp. lemon juice

pinch of hot pepper flakes

METHOD

Dissolve the sugar in the water and then stir in remaining ingredients.

Eggplant Stuffed with Spinach and Goat Cheese

SERVES 4

2 large, firm eggplants

salt

vegetable oil for frying

1-2 cloves garlic, minced

3 cups spinach, washed, stemmed,
   leaves kept whole

1 cup soft, unripened goat cheese,
   crumbled

1/2 cup mozzarella, grated

1/4 cup grated parmesan

2 cups tomato sauce

METHOD

Cut the top and bottom off eggplants, leaving the skin on. Slice lengthwise, about 1/4-inch thick. Line a colander with the eggplant slices, salt them lightly, and let sit for 30 minutes to sweat out bitterness. Pat dry. In a large pan, heat oil and fry the eggplant slices, in batches, adding more oil if necessary. Cook on both sides until browned, then drain on paper towel.

On a flat surface, lay eggplant slices, sprinkle with garlic, cover with spinach leaves, goat cheese, mozzarella, and some of the parmesan. Roll up tightly. Bake at 350° F for 10 minutes until heated through. Meanwhile, heat tomato sauce in a pan. Serve rolls (2 per person) on a pool of tomato sauce and sprinkle with parmesan.

This is an impressive and most delicious appetizer to start a special meal. Great for lunch served with a salad.

Ahmed's Thai Mussels

This recipe was the creation of a most boisterous chef who worked in Grenville's busy kitchen for close to a year. One evening, having just added the hot peppers with his hands, Ahmed had an unbearable urge to relieve himself and ran to the staff washroom. Cries of pain could be heard from the basement as Ahmed had forgotten to wash his hands before peeing. Let's hope he washed them after!

FOR THE PASTE

1 stalk lemon grass, finely chopped, using only the tender parts

2 green onions, finely chopped

1 clove garlic, minced

1 Tbsp. fresh ginger, minced

ground pepper

1/4 tsp. hot pepper flakes

1/2 cup coriander leaves, chopped

METHOD

In a food processor, process all ingredients, reserving 1/3 of the coriander leaves, to a paste. Transfer paste to a small bowl.

FOR 2 SERVINGS OF MUSSELS

2 lb. (about 40) fresh mussels, scrubbed

1 cup canned coconut milk

juice of 1 lime

juice of 1 lemon

a few chili flakes

splash of white wine

2 Tbsp. of the prepared paste

METHOD

In a large, heavy-bottomed pot, place all the ingredients, bring to a boil, covered, and continue cooking until mussels open, about 5 minutes. Place fully opened mussels in a deep bowl, pour sauce over and sprinkle with remaining coriander. Discard any mussels that do not open. Use a large stockpot or 2 separate pans for more than 2 servings.

Crostini with Oyster Mushrooms and Asiago Cheese

**SERVES 2 GENEROUS OR
4 ELEGANT PORTIONS**

1 Tbsp. unsalted butter

3 scallions, chopped

**handful of oyster mushrooms (or any
    mushroom of choice), chopped**

ground pepper, to taste

pinch of salt

dry white wine

METHOD

Sauté all ingredients except wine in a
pan. When mushrooms have browned,
add a splash of white wine to deglaze.
Let the wine bubble for a minute, then
add:

1/4 cup shaved Asiago cheese

1/4 cup whipping cream

Reduce until thick.

Serve on thinly sliced toasted baguette
or bread of your choice. Sprinkle with
fresh parsley or parmesan.

*This is fabulous as a sauce tossed with
pasta or on beef tenderloin for a truly
decadent main course.*

Quesadilla—Two Ways

Black Bean and Corn

3/4 cup dried black beans (turtle beans)

1 bay leaf

1 onion, quartered

1 tsp. ground cumin

1 tsp. chili powder

pinch of hot pepper flakes

6 10-inch flour tortillas

grated Monterey Jack, soft unripened goat
   cheese (optional)

METHOD

Soak the dried black beans overnight
and then cook in a heavy-bottomed pot,
covered generously with water (the
beans absorb a lot of liquid). Cook for
about 1/2 hour, removing foam with a
spoon. (You can substitute canned beans
though the texture will suffer.) Add bay
leaf, onion, and spices. Cover, bring to a
boil, and simmer for about 1 hour until
beans are soft, stirring occasionally.
Strain, removing bay leaf and onion.

In a bowl, mix cooked beans with:

1 fresh jalapeño pepper, chopped

1/2 cup fresh or frozen corn kernels

1/4 cup Three-Pepper Relish (see page 118)
   or prepared salsa

1 heaping tsp. ground cumin

1 heaping tsp. chili powder

1 tsp. thyme

1 tsp. basil

pinch of cayenne

Lay flour tortillas on a counter. Spread
filling generously over the half of each
tortilla. If you wish, sprinkle each with
either Monterey Jack or soft goat cheese
or both. Bake at 350° F on a baking pan
for 10 to 15 minutes, until hot. Cut into
wedges and serve on a chiffonade of
lettuce with your favourite salsa.

*Fold the tortilla in different ways to cre-
ate a burrito or enchilada, as the filling is
suitable for either. Makes a delicious
main course as well.*

Chicken

1 small onion, diced

1/2 sweet pepper, sliced in strips

1 jalapeño pepper, seeded and chopped

1 Tbsp. unsalted butter

pinch of oregano

1 cup cooked chicken meat

4 6-inch flour tortillas or 2 10-inch
   flour tortillas

1/2 cup Monterey Jack cheese or
   cheddar, grated

METHOD

In a frying pan, sauté the onions and peppers in the butter until vegetables begin to soften. Sprinkle with oregano, stir to combine, and remove from heat. Shred cooked chicken into a bowl; add cooked peppers and onions. Lay flour tortillas on a baking sheet and spread some mixture on half of each tortilla. Top with cheese, fold tortillas in half and press down to flatten. Bake at 350° F for about 10 minutes until the melted cheese oozes out. If using large tortillas, cut in wedges to make four appetizer portions. Serve on a chiffonade of lettuce with your favourite salsa.

When we served this dish at The Bookshelf, we spread a thin layer of Coriander Chutney (see page 119) on half of each tortilla, for extra flavour.

Tomato Bruschetta

3 large Roma tomatoes, seeded and diced

2-4 cloves garlic, minced

1/2 red onion, minced

2 Tbsp. olive oil

1 tsp. dried basil or oregano

salt and freshly ground pepper, to taste

METHOD

Toss all ingredients together in a bowl. Set aside for at least 1/2 hour for flavours to blend. Spoon onto toasted baguette.

Three ways to enhance this popular topping are to add crumbled goat cheese to the tomato mixture, spread the baguette with Tapenade, or top with Caponata (see page 121).

Greek Stuffed Summer Tomatoes

The picturesque village of Elora, a short drive from Guelph, became a fashionable tourist location in the early '80s. One reason for its success was an eclectic French restaurant called Café Flore, presided over by its two lively owners, Floreal and Rita. Written in bold letters was the café's motto, "If You're in a Hurry … Forget It!" Their large display case featured many memorable items, but the most striking was a sumptuously stuffed tomato, which is the inspiration for the recipe that follows.

FOR 4 SERVINGS

4 large vine-ripened tomatoes

1/2 cup feta cheese, thinly sliced

1/4 red onion, thinly sliced

**1/2 cucumber, sliced (English or local
summer-fresh)**

12 kalamata olives, pitted and chopped

extra-virgin olive oil

juice of one lemon

**1 tsp. dried oregano or 1/2 cup fresh basil,
chopped**

black pepper

METHOD

Slice the top off the tomatoes and make 4-6 parallel slits 3/4 of the way through the flesh. Be sure that the tomato stays whole. Fill the 4 slits with very thin slices of feta cheese, red onion, and cucumber. Distribute the feta, onion, and cucumbers evenly. The tomato will fan out and look impressive. Sprinkle olives over each tomato. Drizzle with extra-virgin olive oil, lemon juice, a pinch of oregano or fresh basil, and a generous grind of black pepper. One tomato per person makes a great starter for a summer barbecue.

Avocado, Endive, and Grapefruit with Citrus Honey Mustard Vinaigrette

The dressing for this salad has been the "house" dressing at The Bookshelf Café for years. We use dozens of oranges and lemons daily, plus a hand blender the size of a jack-hammer to keep up with the demand. This salad is our favourite way to start a dinner party at home. It presents beautifully, is a wonderful combination of flavours, and leaves plenty of room for what follows.

FOR 4 SALADS

Assemble on a large serving platter or on individual salad plates:

leaves of 2 large belgian endive

1 firm, ripe avocado, peeled and cut into thin wedges

1 large, pink grapefruit, peeled and sectioned (juice reserved)

a handful of sliced almonds, toasted (optional)

CITRUS HONEY MUSTARD VINAIGRETTE

juice of 1 lemon

juice of 1 orange

1 Tbsp. honey mustard

reserved grapefruit juice

splash of balsamic vinegar

pinch of dried tarragon

ground pepper, to taste

1/2 cup canola oil or light olive oil

METHOD

Whisk together all vinaigrette ingredients, saving the oil for last. If you prefer a thick dressing, use a hand blender or a food processor. Drizzle the oil in slowly, whisking quickly, to emulsify.

Spoon dressing over assembled salad. Sprinkle with almonds for an extra treat.

To toast almonds, place on a baking sheet in a 350° F oven (or toaster oven) for about 10 minutes until golden brown and aromatic.

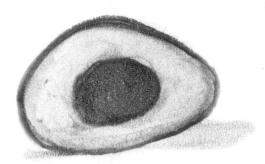

Cleopatra Salad

The public health department of Ottawa-Carleton put out a warning in the early '90s concerning the danger of using raw eggs to make Caesar salad. Apparently, a number of restaurant diners had contracted salmonella poisoning from eating this most popular salad, and the health department insisted that establishments coddle the eggs to destroy bacteria, or better still, use "egg replacers" as a substitute. Never huge fans of the Caesar to begin with, and appalled by the idea of substitutions, we at Grenville's decided to invent a salad that had similar qualities to the Caesar without the threat. Thus the name.

FOR 4 SALADS

1 large head romaine lettuce, hearts and
    nicest greens cleaned and spun dry
1 cup prepared croutons, see recipe

FOR THE DRESSING

1/4 cup dry sun-dried tomatoes, soaked in
    boiling water
2 cloves garlic, crushed
1 tsp. dry mustard
1/4 cup parmesan, grated
3 Tbsp. balsamic vinegar
1/4 cup olive oil
a few twists of black pepper

METHOD

Strain the softened tomatoes and save the liquid. In a food processor, purée the tomatoes, garlic, mustard, parmesan, and balsamic vinegar. Add some of the reserved liquid if the mixture is dry. With the machine running, drizzle in olive oil to emulsify. Add pepper.

FOR THE CROUTONS

day-old baguette or Italian bread
2 Tbsp. olive oil
1 pinch each of: oregano, thyme, garlic
    powder, salt, fresh ground pepper

METHOD

Remove crust from bread and cut into cubes. Toss in a bowl with olive oil, oregano, thyme, garlic powder, salt, and a few grinds of black pepper. Bake on a baking sheet at 300° F for 10 to 15 minutes. The croutons should be crisp and golden.

To finish the salad, toss the romaine with the croutons and the dressing, 1 tablespoon at a time. Toss, toss, and toss, adding a bit of parmesan if you wish, until the lettuce is well coated. Serve with a lemon wedge per plate.

Cobb Salad with Ranch Dressing

This salad works very well as a sandwich filling if you cut the vegetables smaller and mix the salad with the dressing. For a salad, just combine the following ingredients and place them on a bed of your favourite greens.

FOR 4 SALADS

6 strips of bacon, cooked crisp and chopped

4 hard-boiled eggs, cut in quarters

3 ripe tomatoes, cut in wedges

1 ripe avocado, cut in chunks

1 sweet pepper, chopped

1 small red onion, cut in rings

RANCH DRESSING

Whisk together or process with a hand blender:

2/3 cup buttermilk

1 cup mayonnaise

juice of 1/2 lemon

1/2 small onion, grated

1 clove garlic, minced

1/3 cup fresh dill, chopped

3 sprigs fresh parsley, chopped

several twists of freshly ground pepper

METHOD

Gently toss bacon, eggs, tomatoes, avocado, and peppers with enough dressing to coat (this recipe makes more than you'll need). Place on prepared salad plates and garnish with red onion rings.

This salad is delicious with crumbled blue cheese. The extra dressing will keep in the refrigerator and is great as a dip for veggies, baked as a glaze for fish, or as an everyday, all-purpose salad dressing.

Laura's Holiday Salad

My sister-in-law, Laura DiVilio, is a wonderful cook who brings imagination and grace to all her meals. Cooking is an art form to Laura, and she has been known to labour for days to create the perfect dinner. The fact that we are professionals has caused alarm to many friends who are too intimidated to cook for us. Not so Laura, who, having worked in restaurants herself, knows how much we appreciate being fed by others.

The salad that follows can be made to feed a crowd at Thanksgiving or any other large family holiday. The ingredients have so much flavour that the dressing is as simple as can be.

1 medium radicchio, shredded

12 cups salad greens including arugula and endive

1 small fennel bulb, thinly sliced

1 cup walnuts, roasted and chopped

1 large pomegranate, seeds only

1 firm Bosc pear, thinly sliced (optional)

extra-virgin olive oil

red wine vinegar

salt and pepper, to taste

METHOD

Place salad ingredients in a large bowl and drizzle with olive oil, toss, then drizzle with red wine vinegar, then sprinkle with salt and toss again. Twist generous amounts of black pepper over the salad and toss again. This is truly a tossed salad and the technique works to bring all the flavours into play.

THE BISTRO LUNCH

SALADS AS A MEAL

Salad Song

Deluxe Salad—revisited

Smoked Salmon Salad with Apples and
  Blue Cheese Scallion Dressing

Vegetable Kebabs with Roasted
  Garlic Dressing

Asian Marinated Chicken Salad with
  Sesame Ginger Dressing

Salade Niçoise

Warm Goat Cheese on a Bed of Greens
  with Herb Balsamic Vinaigrette

Warm Salmon Salad with Lemon Pepper
  Vinaigrette

SIMPLE ENTRÉES

Gatineau Hills

Orange Dijon Chicken

Gatineau Hills Baked Chicken

Honey Chili Roast Chicken

Chicken Enchiladas Rio Grande

Mexican Shepherd's Pie

Seafood "Annie Savoy"

Spinach and Chevre Tart

Spinach and Feta Strudel

Jambalaya

SANDWICHES

Counter Intelligence

The Reuben

Grilled Ham and Brie

Curried Chicken Salad

The New Yorker

Bistro Club Croissant

Vegetarian Fajita Sandwich

Roasted Vegetable Sandwich—Two Ways

Greek Pizza with Tapenade

SALADS AS A MEAL

Salad Song

The perfect summer meal for someone who works in a steamy restaurant kitchen, sweat dripping from wrinkled brow, air thick enough to push aside, is, without a doubt, a great big salad. Crisp summer greens, luscious vine-ripened tomatoes, and sweet young onions untouched by a flicker of flame revive a wilting chef. How civilized it would be to simply offer a room temperature menu and extinguish the burners, silence the fryer, still the mighty salamander, and grill no more.

Tastes often change when summer heat first arrives. Like a New Year's resolution, the season can inspire diners to banish old habits and eat lighter, share appetizers perhaps, or even forgo red meat for fish. Even the most dyed-in-the-wool carnivore can be tempted by the joys of fresh asparagus or sugar snap peas. Sadly, as the days grow longer and the winter becomes a vague, unpleasant memory, old habits return with appetites that crave the kinds of food that need fire and plenty of it. Alas, we cannot cook summer meats outside like macho barbecuers, apron wrapped, and brandishing tools like sabers. Trapped indoors, experiencing hot flashes that last for hours, we dream of the cool gin and tonic just beyond our reach. If the world were a kinder place, then come spring, a person's fancy would turn to salad and make life easy for those of us who cook for a living. In our opinion, self-serving as it may be, there is nothing finer than any of the following salads, each a meal in itself and requiring as little heat as possible.

Deluxe Salad—revisited

This recipe was a favourite at The Baker Street Bistro and appeared in our first cookbook under the same name. We have changed certain ingredients and think it is worthy of inclusion again, as it is a most perfect and satisfying meal.

FOR 4 SALADS

Arrange on a large platter, in a salad bowl, or on 4 individual plates:

1 head of lettuce (romaine, leaf, Boston, or any combination), washed and torn

2 tomatoes, cut in wedges

1 English cucumber, sliced

1 sweet pepper, seeded and thinly sliced

1 small carrot, grated

1 avocado, cut in chunks

1 handful of almonds, slivered or sliced and toasted

1 cup feta cheese, crumbled

METHOD

Arrange the salad in any manner that suits, topping with crumbled feta and toasted almonds. Drizzle with Bistro Vinaigrette, which dates back to our childhood.

BISTRO VINAIGRETTE

1 cup oil, olive or vegetable

1/2 cup red wine vinegar

1 Tbsp. ketchup

1/2 tsp. dry mustard or 1 tsp. Dijon or honey mustard

pinch of granulated sugar

pinch of salt

pinch of garlic powder

2 grinds of ground pepper

lemon juice (optional)

METHOD

Shake all ingredients together in a covered jar and taste. You may want to adjust the ratio of oil to vinegar.

Smoked Salmon Salad with Apples and Blue Cheese Scallion Dressing

Whenever it is time to change a menu, there is always a hue and cry from customers regarding the loss of certain dishes. Vivvette Carew, a long-time server and friend, approached me recently and warned that her clientele would be upset if I removed the Smoked Salmon Salad from the menu. I have always considered this to be one of our best salads, but was not convinced that the public felt the same way. Not long after the warning, I came across Vivvette and her young son Evan chowing down on said dish and immediately understood the particular clients she was referring to.

FOR 4 SALADS

6 cups spring mix or a comparable amount of salad greens including leaf lettuce, frisée, Boston lettuce, arugula, and radicchio

1 small red onion, sliced

1/4 lb. sliced smoked salmon, divided in small pieces

1 large tart apple, peeled and sliced

METHOD

Toss all ingredients together in a bowl with Blue Cheese Scallion Dressing.

BLUE CHEESE SCALLION DRESSING

1/2 cup sour cream

1/2 cup blue cheese, crumbled

1 cup mayonnaise

1/3 cup white wine vinegar

2-3 drops Tabasco sauce

splash of Worcestershire sauce

3 green onions, chopped

ground black pepper, to taste

METHOD

Whisk all ingredients together. The dressing will be lumpy from the cheese.

This recipe makes a great dip for crudités or Chicken Sesame (see page 27) and can be used as an all-purpose blue cheese dressing. At the Paramount Café, we used a combination of Boston lettuce, orange sections, toasted sunflower seeds, and red onions, tossed it with the dressing and had great results.

Vegetable Kebabs with Roasted Garlic Dressing

FOR 4 SERVINGS

1 zucchini, cut in 1-inch chunks

8 cherry tomatoes

1 onion, cut in 8 wedges

8 mushrooms, wiped clean

1 small red bell pepper, seeded and
  cut in chunks

1 large head Boston or leaf lettuce or
  6 cups spring mix

olive oil for brushing

8 wooden skewers

METHOD

Use any mix of lettuces for this salad.
Divide the vegetables and thread on
8 wooden skewers that have been
soaked in water for at least 10 minutes.
Brush with olive oil and grill or barbecue
for 2 to 3 minutes per side. Place skewered vegetables on a bed of lettuce (or
remove from skewers before serving if
you wish) and drizzle with Roasted Garlic
Dressing.

ROASTED GARLIC DRESSING

1 whole garlic bulb, top 1/2 inch cut off

1 ripe tomato

1 Tbsp. Dijon mustard

2-3 drops Tabasco sauce

1/4 cup red wine vinegar

splash of Worcestershire sauce

1/2 tsp. dry or 1 Tbsp. fresh rosemary

ground black pepper, a generous amount

1/2 cup olive oil

METHOD

In a baking pan, roast the garlic with the
tomato at 400° F for 1/2 hour. The tomato will shed its skin, and the garlic will
begin to ooze. Squeeze the garlic from
its skin and place in the bowl of a food
processor (or use a hand blender). Add
the roasted tomato, coarsely chopped.
Purée with the mustard, Tabasco, vinegar, Worcestershire, rosemary, and pepper, slowly drizzling in olive oil until thick.

Asian Marinated Chicken Salad with Sesame Ginger Dressing

FOR 4 SALADS

1 Tbsp. fresh coriander, chopped

1 Tbsp. fresh ginger, grated

2 Tbsp. soy sauce

splash of sesame oil

1 Tbsp. olive oil

4 boneless, skinless chicken breasts
(2, halved, for appetizer portions)

METHOD

Whisk together all ingredients, except chicken breasts. Pour over chicken breasts and marinate for at least 10 minutes or as long as overnight. Remove chicken from marinade and grill, broil, or bake until done.

THE SALAD

1 large carrot, grated

1/2 small Napa cabbage, shredded

1 large handful of bean sprouts

1 small head romaine or leaf lettuce, torn
or in chiffonade

2 green onions, chopped

1/2 cup coriander leaves, torn (optional)

METHOD

Toss the salad ingredients together with the dressing and distribute evenly among 4 large plates. Top with cooked chicken breast, sliced and still hot. Drizzle cooking juices or extra dressing on top.

SESAME GINGER DRESSING

Whisk together:

1 Tbsp. ginger, grated

1 Tbsp. honey mustard

1 tsp. sesame oil

1 Tbsp. soy sauce

juice of one lime

juice of one orange

1/4 tsp. hot sauce (optional)

1/2 cup olive oil

Thin rice vermicelli crisp up like magic, straight from the package, when cooked in hot oil. In a wok, heat 2 to 3 inches of vegetable or canola oil until very hot. Test with one noodle. If it puffs up instantly, the oil is hot enough. Carefully place a small handful of noodles into the hot wok and remove immediately with a slotted spoon to a bowl lined with paper towel. Repeat twice to have more than enough crispy noodles to top 4 salads.

Salade Niçoise

FOR 4 SALADS

4 eggs, hard-boiled and quartered

4 new potatoes, boiled

**1 1/2 cups green beans or asparagus,
blanched**

2-3 ripe tomatoes, cut in wedges

**1 sweet bell pepper, yellow, red, or green,
seeded and cut in strips**

1 small cucumber, sliced

1 head lettuce

1 small red onion, cut in rings

20 kalamata olives

**1 can tuna or 8 oz. piece of fresh tuna,
grilled**

METHOD

On 4 individual plates, make a bed of
lettuce and divide the rest of the ingredients, arranging them equally between
the four salads. If using canned tuna,
strain the oil or water and crumble the
tuna over the salads. If grilling or barbe-
cuing fresh tuna, remove from heat
before fish is cooked through, slice into
1/4-inch pieces and distribute. Drizzle
with your favourite dressing and serve.

DRESSING SUGGESTIONS
Herb Balsamic (see page 48), Lemon
Pepper (see page 49) or Bistro
Vinaigrette (see page 43).

*In order to keep beans and asparagus
crisp and brilliant in colour, plunge them
into a bowl of ice water after removing
from heat. Wax beans and sugar snap
peas can be substituted, as can cooked
shrimp or grilled chicken.*

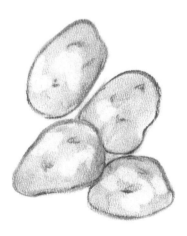

Warm Goat Cheese on a Bed of Greens with Herb Balsamic Vinaigrette

FOR 4 SERVINGS

8 oz. soft unripened goat cheese

olive oil

1/4 cup ground pecans, almonds, walnuts,
  or combination

6 cups spring mix or any combination of
  salad greens

1 small red onion, cut into thin rings

METHOD

Divide goat cheese into 4 equal-size balls and flatten them in your palm to form pucks. Place a small amount of olive oil in a bowl and roll goat cheese pucks in oil to coat. Place nuts in a small bowl and roll cheese pucks until generously covered. Place on plate covered with waxed paper. When you are ready to assemble the salads, heat the goat cheese pucks on a baking sheet at 350° F for 5 to 10 minutes or until warmed through.

Meanwhile, toss greens and onion rings with enough dressing to coat and distribute equally on 4 large plates. Place warmed goat cheese atop salads and serve. For a delicious taste treat, top "pucks" with Coriander Chutney (see page 119).

HERB BALSAMIC VINAIGRETTE

2 cups fresh herbs, combination of basil,
  rosemary, thyme, parsley, dill, or
  basil alone

1 clove garlic, minced

1 Tbsp. granulated sugar

1 Tbsp. Dijon mustard

1/4 cup balsamic vinegar

2 Tbsp. rice wine vinegar (optional)

ground black pepper, to taste

1 1/2 cups vegetable or olive oil

METHOD

With a hand blender or food processor, combine herbs, garlic, sugar, and mustard until they form a paste. With the machine running, add vinegar(s) and slowly drizzle in oil until dressing is emulsified. Add ground pepper to taste. You will have more dressing than you need. Reserve extra for use as an excellent all-purpose dressing.

Warm Salmon Salad with Lemon Pepper Vinaigrette

FOR 4 SERVINGS

4 6 oz. salmon fillets

salt and pepper, to taste

juice of 1 lemon

6 cups baby spinach

METHOD

To prepare this excellent dinner salad, grill, bake, or broil salmon fillets that have been lightly seasoned with salt, ground pepper, and lemon juice. When firm but not dry, place on a bed of baby spinach that has been tossed with Lemon Pepper Vinaigrette. Top with a dollop of Tartar Sauce.

LEMON PEPPER VINAIGRETTE

1/8 cup red wine vinegar

rind of 1 lemon, grated

2 lemons, juiced

2 sprigs parsley, chopped

1 Tbsp. mint, chopped

pinch of salt

fresh ground pepper, lots!

1/4 cup olive oil

METHOD

Place vinegar, lemon juice and rind, parsley, mint, salt, and pepper in a bowl. Whisk in olive oil until thickened.

TARTAR SAUCE

3/4 cup mayonnaise

1/4 cup prepared, store-bought, sweet green relish

juice of 1 lemon

METHOD

Mix all ingredients.

At The Bookshelf, we serve this simple salad with Tomato Bruschetta (see page 34), which makes it a perfect one-course meal.

SANDWICHES

Counter Intelligence

No matter how long one works in a chosen profession, it is inevitable that one day a new challenge will arise that is cause for alarm. When Glenna and I decided to throw our lot in with the folks at The Bookshelf Café, we knew that circumstance might require one or both of us to perform duties that were not part of our past, owner-based, reality.

Working for someone else is a whole different kettle of fish. For one thing, you get paid! For another, you are no longer master of your own destiny. Even though the position of "manager" implies certain autonomy, there is now a "boss," who didn't factor into the equation when you owned your own business. Said individual makes decisions that aren't always exactly what you had in mind.

Not long after we had established ourselves in The Bookshelf's cozy back dining room, an ownership-inspired renovation created a small café at the very front of the bookstore, facing Quebec Street. The person serving the new area would also make sandwiches, salads, and other items that were to be listed on the giant blackboards. As this was a totally new position, I decided to be the first to take on the job of "counter-boy."

Years ago, in Toronto, I used to go for Saturday breakfast at a place called The Crescent Grill on Spadina Avenue. The short-order cook who worked the counter performed tasks with the grace of a dancer and looked a lot like a working-class Peter O'Toole. He would crack eggs and hurl the shells behind him into the waiting garbage without even looking. Slicing bagels, flipping pancakes, refilling coffee, and handling dozens of orders at the same time seemed like a piece of cake to this maestro. Take away the grill, the watery blue eyes, and the eggshells, and you have some idea of how I tried to romanticize my new position.

Delusions of grandeur you might think! Well, after all this time, I was entitled to a little fantasizing when faced with a job like this. I was well aware that "nuke-ing" a piece of lasagna for three minutes wasn't eggs over easy with crispy bacon, home fries, and brown toast, but I was getting pretty good at throwing empty pop cans into the garbage.

I bet the Spadina guy didn't have to make a skinny decaf cappuccino (was that cinnamon or chocolate?), or a chai latte with soy. And nobody ever talked to him, they just watched in admiration.

Unfortunately, my performance did not inspire awe, and clients felt more than free to tell me their problems, visions, desires—you name it. I was a standing duck! There was really no place to hide, and so I had to try to be pleasant (not my natural state) as I handled all the demands of the job. Standing out front, apron-clad, tongs poised, tray in hand, I often wondered how I got myself in this position to begin with. It must have been karma!

From my childhood days in Manhattan, I remember various wise guys in stained aprons, swearing behind counters or calling over grease-covered cooks to have a laugh at what some schmuck from Jersey had just said. These guys were tough, and, as a little kid tagging along with the workers on a break from my Uncle Sol's stuffed-toy factory, they both thrilled and scared me. How was I to know that one day I would end up doing the same job?

The big difference is that the smart-ass remarks I think of serving along with the herb tea and currant scones wouldn't go over quite as well as they did in the Bowery. After all, this ain't Flatbush Avenue, and sarcasm isn't exactly mother's milk to the average Guelphite. There's also the little problem of public relations. Nasty doesn't fly in "granola-ville!"

So, after sober second thoughts, I decided to retire from working the counter. I'm pretty good at it, but holding my tongue was starting to get to me. So were the lousy tips. Better to let somebody younger, with a different frame of reference and a sweeter disposition, do the job.

The Reuben

One of the more trying aspects of our work at *The Bookshelf* is the policy of feeding staff for half price. This "staff benefit" is a bonus to booksellers and cinema ushers, but at peak hours, can wreak havoc on the kitchen. Why bring lunch when you can eat what you like for next to nothing and have it made for you? If I sound mean-spirited, it's because, much like spoiled children, the staff believe that they're entitled to this perk and hardly, if ever, express a hint of appreciation for the food it takes the kitchen time and care to prepare.

The Bookshelf's reputation as an alternative haven of nutrition and spirituality would be savaged by the food tastes of its employees. Scratch a bookseller and you'll find a carnivore of the first order. A Reuben sandwich, which is meat, cheese, and Dijonnaise, is a staff favourite, especially when fries accompany it. So much for new-age tastes! Sometimes I feel, if it were up to me, the food service staff would eat for free, and everyone else would pay for day-old muffins.

FOR 1 SANDWICH

2 thick slices of challah (egg bread) or rye
2-3 slices corned beef
2 slices Swiss or cheddar cheese
1 Tbsp. Dijonnaise: 1 part mayo,
  1 part dijon
sauerkraut, to taste

METHOD

You can make this sandwich just like grilled cheese, by buttering a heavy skillet and frying the sandwich on both sides until golden and the cheese is melted. Alternatively, it can be baked open-faced at 375° F, one side with sauerkraut and meat, the other with the cheese. Bake until the cheese melts and then close the sandwich and slice.

A pleasant variation would be caramelized onions as a substitute for sauerkraut.

Grilled Ham and Brie

Where sandwiches are concerned, old standards often prove to be very popular. Fads come and go, but familiar comfort foods still hold their ground with the average diner. Using Brie in this sandwich re-invents it just enough to please those who are looking for something new but not too much to scare off timid conservatives. It is our best seller.

FOR 1 SANDWICH

2 thick slices of challah (egg bread)

honey mustard

2 slices of ham (your favourite)

2 generous slices of Brie, chilled before
   slicing

unsalted butter

METHOD

Spread a little honey mustard on each slice of bread. Layer one slice with ham and the other with Brie. Close sandwich. Lightly butter the outside of the sandwich and, in a flat-bottomed heavy pan, fry until golden. Then flip it over and fry the other side. This sandwich can also be baked open-faced, removed from oven, closed, and sliced.

Sauté white part of leeks in unsalted butter and place on top of ham before closing the sandwich and grilling. The leeks add a delicious dimension to the sandwich.

Curried Chicken Salad

This dish has been a staple since the very early days of the Baker Street Bistro. It began its life as a filling for croissants, was deep-fried in egg roll wrappers, and reborn as an elegant appetizer called "autumn rolls." It is a menu workhorse like none other. After serving it for 20 years, I have no problem admitting that I could eat it every day. Not a bad recommendation!

SERVES 4-6

2 thighs and 2 breasts of chicken

1 stalk celery, cut in half

1 carrot, cut in thirds

1 clove garlic

1 onion, cut in quarters

6 peppercorns

2 sprigs parsley (optional)

METHOD

Place all ingredients in a large pot of water, cover, bring to a boil, and simmer for about an hour until chicken is cooked. Strain and reserve stock for another purpose.

When chicken has cooled, remove skin and bones and either shred or cut the chicken into fair-size pieces.

DRESSING

1 stalk celery, diced

2 green onions, chopped

1 cup mayonnaise (or to taste)

1 heaping Tbsp. marmalade or fruit chutney

2 Tbsp. curry powder, or more to taste

1/2 cup toasted almonds, slivered or sliced

In a bowl, gently mix together all ingredients with the cooled chicken until blended.

The New Yorker

This sandwich got its name because of the pairing of smoked turkey with Russian dressing. Normally served on rye bread with plenty of caraway seeds, this is a very traditional New York deli classic.

FOR 1 SANDWICH

1 bagel, sliced and toasted

3 slices smoked turkey

1 slice Swiss cheese

**1/8 cup Russian dressing: equal parts
    mayonnaise and chili sauce**

lettuce

sliced tomato

sliced red onion

METHOD

Take 1 slice of the toasted bagel and pile the turkey and Swiss cheese on top of a piece of lettuce. Slather with some dressing and garnish with tomato and red onion.

Bistro Club Croissant

Nicolino Giardino, a long-time customer, friend, and, most importantly, hair stylist, likes to reminisce about certain foods we used to serve in the "good old days." His mother, Ada, is a magnificent cook in the Southern Italian tradition, and Nic considers his taste, in all things, to be exquisite.

After a long evening of dinner and good red wine, he is likely to start rambling about "that great sandwich you used to serve, back in the '80s, at the Bistro." My eyes begin to roll as he sings the praises of the Club Croissant, as if he's never enlightened me about it before. In fact, he's probably mourned the loss of this particular item at least 100 times, and it's only the length of our friendship and my daughters' addiction to his talents, that has kept me from strangling him in order to get him to shut up about it.

We used to go to Patachou, in Toronto, to get the croissants that helped make this sandwich unforgettable. Despite the fact that bagels and wraps have replaced the rich, buttery French pastry as the sandwich bread of choice, I suggest that you use only the best croissants available when making this club.

FOR EACH CROISSANT

2 strips bacon, crispy

1 slice tomato

2 oz. cooked chicken, sliced

2 slices avocado

1 lettuce leaf

METHOD

Spread each half of the croissant with basil mayonnaise to taste. Then stack all ingredients and close sandwich.

FOR THE BASIL MAYO

1/4 cup mayonnaise

1 tsp. chopped fresh basil

ground black pepper, to taste

splash of red wine vinegar

METHOD

Mix all ingredients together and eat to your arteries' content.

Vegetarian Fajita Sandwich

TO MAKE 4 SANDWICHES

1 bell pepper, seeded

1 stalk of celery

1 small carrot

1 small onion

1 small zucchini

1 jalapeño pepper, seeded (optional)

1/2 tsp. chili powder

1/2 tsp. ground cumin

1/2 tsp. ground coriander

1/2 tsp. dried oregano

salt and pepper, to taste

splash of olive oil

splash of lemon juice

4 large (10-inch) flour tortillas

4 Tbsp. salsa, bought or homemade

METHOD

Julienne all the vegetables and toss in a bowl with spices, herbs, oil, and lemon juice. Marinate at room temperature for approximately 1/2 hour.

Stir-fry vegetables in a wok or frying pan until hot but still crisp. Spread each flour tortilla with 1 tablespoon salsa (see page 122). Mound 1/4 of the vegetable mixture at one end of the tortilla and roll it up. Bake at 350° F briefly if the vegetables are still hot, or longer if they have cooled. Cut in half and serve.

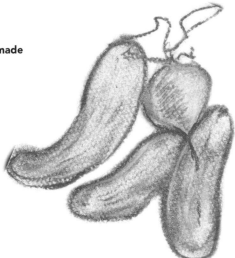

Roasted Vegetable Sandwich—Two Ways

TO MAKE 1 SANDWICH

1 zucchini, sliced lengthwise

1 sweet red pepper, seeded and halved

1 onion, halved

1 eggplant, sliced (optional)

olive oil

METHOD

Place vegetables in a pan, drizzle with olive oil, and roast at 400° F for about 20 minutes. Remove from the oven, skin pepper, and chop all the vegetables.

   Spread a 10-inch flour tortilla generously with one of the following spreads, top with chopped vegetables, and roll up to form a "wrap."

HUMMUS

2 cloves garlic

1 19 oz. can chickpeas, drained, liquid reserved

2 heaping Tbsp. tahini (sesame paste)

juice of 1 lemon

pinch of cayenne

1/2 tsp. basil

1/2 tsp. cumin

a few twists of black pepper

METHOD

In a blender or food processor, purée with some of the reserved liquid until creamy.

HERBED GOAT CHEESE

1 cup soft goat cheese

1 Tbsp. Basil Pesto (see page 116)

METHOD

Blend to combine.

If you have a barbecue, you can grill the vegetables rather than bake them, for comparable results.

Greek Pizza with Tapenade

FOR 4 SANDWICHES

4 Greek-style pitas

Tapenade

1 bell pepper (red, green, or a combination), seeded and thinly sliced

1 small red onion, cut into rings

2 large tomatoes, sliced

1 cup feta, crumbled

1/2 cup mozzarella, grated

dried oregano

METHOD

Spread 4 pitas with tapenade and distribute the peppers, onions, and tomatoes equally. Top with feta, then mozzarella, and sprinkle with oregano to taste. Bake at 400° F for 5 to 7 minutes until cheese is bubbling and slightly browned.

TAPENADE

1 cup kalamata olives, pitted

1 Tbsp. capers, chopped

2 cloves garlic, chopped

2 Tbsp. olive oil

splash of lemon juice

METHOD

Blend the olives, capers, and garlic together in a food processor. Add remaining ingredients and process to make a paste.

You will have more tapenade than you need. Save covered in the refrigerator and use as a delicious addition to pasta sauces, mixed with goat cheese for a sandwich spread, or as a traditional pizza topping.

SIMPLE ENTRÉES

Gatineau Hills

Econiche House in the Gatineau is a rustic retreat and conference centre 30 minutes north of Ottawa. Up a winding, narrow highway, bordered by maple bush, and opening to broad vistas of the log-jammed Cantley River, Econiche sits, carved out of the bush, like a homemade, wooden fortress. Dr. Brian Bailey, a disheveled bear-like man, consumed with new-age philosophy, built his dream lodge to facilitate groups of individuals seeking a path to spiritual awareness. He also booked conference facilities and overnight rooms to some civil servants and other government-associated types who needed to brainstorm and get down to the business of running the country. Econiche offered privacy and a change of scenery. For three years, in addition to the grueling task of running Grenville's, I drove up that mountain and became chief cook and bottle-washer to the truth seekers, both spiritual and political, who frequented Econiche.

Early most mornings, I would check in at the restaurant, jump into my car and head for the hills. Speeding over the border into Quebec always caused me a touch of anxiety. Inevitably in a hurry, driving a car with too much horsepower, I dreaded being stopped by the local police authority, whom I assumed would speak only French. "Est-ce que vous voulez quelque chose à boire?" or "Desirez-vous une desserte?" were hardly adequate responses when being pulled over for speeding. Waiting on tables in downtown Ottawa had improved my restaurant French tremendously, but I was tongue-tied by everyday parlance. I was always in too much of a hurry to obey the law. As well, the locals drove like maniacs, no matter what the weather, so despite my fears and anxiety, I would make the drive in record time.

The kitchen at Econiche is a cook's dream. Large windows overlook the tops of tall trees with the beautiful river in the distance. Entering my domain every morning was always a pleasure no matter how hectic the schedule, because it was so quiet. Serving breakfast to overnight guests was the responsibility of Brian and the housekeeping staff, so my chores included morning snack (like a daycare centre), preparing, serving, and cleaning up lunch, and cooking the supper that would be served by a local farm woman. During my first year, I would prepare the two snacks and both meals, be finished by 11:30 a.m., hop back into my car and drive to Grenville's in time to serve lunch. Looking back, I can't believe I did it. But times were hard for us back then, and this was a lucrative business.

One of the most interesting aspects of my time in the Gatineau was the different types of people to be fed. In one week alone, I might be serving a group from the Council of Canadians, the Federal Department of Communications including the Deputy Minister, a national meeting of native leaders or the followers of some obscure American meditation guru. Through the kitchen door, I might hear chanting one day or a motivational speaker the next. People's eating habits were as diverse as their agendas. When an organization reserved accommodation, they chose from a catering menu that was sent with the brochure. Groups that made strict dietary demands were almost always hungrier than the guys in suits. Greedier too! Certain leaders would dictate the number of times when participants could eat, and people would almost trample each other to get to the food. I'm willing to bet that the personal mantra for most of these fasting meditations was, "Feed me! Feed me! Feed me!" The government bigwigs, on the other hand, expected the food in this primitive, out-of-the-way location, to be lousy, and when it wasn't, they were thrilled.

I learned a lot about myself during my tenure at Econiche House. Owning a restaurant, despite its service component, is far more glamorous than standing behind a counter and dishing up a casserole. The people I was serving were my contemporaries, but on bad days my job seemed mighty insignificant compared with theirs. Believe me when I say that I have nothing but respect for the work I do, but it is of a servile nature and at Econiche, there was no way of hiding it. There were days when I wanted to throw off my apron, jump over the counter, sit down, and chant or brainstorm, or do anything but the dishes. Then I would smarten up, look around, and see the job for what it was. Feeding people well is simple, good work that makes sense. Many of the people I was serving had jobs that were all talk, that were full of frustration and contradiction and compromise. Though humbled, I could feel good about what I did.

I consider my time spent at Econiche House to be particularly sweet. The food I cooked was honest, tasty, nutritious, and very economical to make. I kept my food costs to around 15 percent, half of what a restaurant aspires to, and made a ton of money that Grenville's, the bottomless pit, greedily consumed. To Brian Bailey, his wife Nancy, Dave, the wonderful Thérèse Chartrand, her husband, Johnny, Helene, Ruth, Jeff Leney, and everyone I worked with in the hills of Quebec, I give my heartfelt "merci" for sharing a most precious part of my professional journey.

The three recipes that follow are examples of the quick and easy food that I served at Econiche.

1 chicken cut in pieces, or just your favourite parts

Orange Dijon Chicken

1/4 cup Dijon mustard

1/4 cup orange marmalade

a splash of soy sauce

a pinch of curry powder

METHOD

Assemble chicken pieces on a baking sheet, season with salt and ground pepper. Combine sauce ingredients and generously spread some of the mixture on chicken. Bake at 375° F for 30 minutes. Baste with more sauce, and bake for another 15 minutes or until pieces are golden brown.

Gatineau Hills Baked Chicken

1/4 cup Dijon mustard

1/4 cup sour cream or yogourt

1 Tbsp. mayonnaise

salt and ground pepper, to taste

1 cup breadcrumbs

METHOD

Combine Dijon, sour cream, and mayonnaise. Sprinkle chicken with salt and pepper, dredge in the mustard mixture, and let sit at room temperature for 10 to 15 minutes. Roll in breadcrumbs and bake at 375° F for 45 minutes or until pieces are golden brown and cooked through.

Honey Chili Roast Chicken

2 Tbsp. olive oil

1 tsp. thyme leaves

1 clove garlic, minced

salt and pepper, to taste

1/4 cup honey

1 Tbsp. lemon juice

2 Tbsp. Dijon mustard

2 Tbsp. garlic chili sauce (available in Asian markets and many supermarkets)

METHOD

Mix olive oil, thyme, garlic, salt, and pepper. Rub on chicken pieces and set aside. Combine honey, lemon juice, Dijon, and garlic chili sauce. Dredge chicken pieces in mixture, spoon more sauce over, and bake at 375° F for 30 minutes. Baste with more sauce and bake 15 minutes longer.

Chicken Enchiladas Rio Grande

SERVES 4 (2 ROLLS PER PERSON)

If there is a recipe that I would consider an old workhorse, it is the filling for these enchiladas. We have used this filling as a sauce over chicken breasts stuffed with cheese and rolled in cornmeal, as an appetizer crostini on toasted baguette, or tossed with pasta. It is all-purpose and good with just about anything—except ice cream!

1 large onion, thinly sliced

2 bell peppers, red, green or yellow, cut in
   thin strips

1 Tbsp. unsalted butter

1 pickled jalapeño pepper, seeded and
   chopped

1 Tbsp. oregano

1/2 cup whipping cream

4 cups cooked chicken, shredded or cut in
   large pieces

2 cups Monterey Jack cheese, grated

8 6-inch flour tortillas

METHOD

In a large frying pan, slowly simmer the onions and peppers in the butter, stirring often, until very soft. Sprinkle with oregano, add the heavy cream and reduce until thickened. Stir in chicken and cheese, leaving some cheese for the top. Divide filling equally between tortillas and roll up into tube-like enchiladas. Sprinkle the extra cheese on top and bake at 350° F for 10 minutes. Serve with green salad and your favourite salsa.

Mexican Shepherd's Pie

Re-inventing an old standby is always pleasurable. What could be more familiar than shepherd's pie? In this update, we've taken an old Mexican classic called Picadillo and topped it with a sweet potato mash and presto—something totally new.

1 onion, chopped

1 clove garlic, minced

1 Tbsp. olive oil

1 lb. extra lean ground beef

1 16 oz. can diced tomatoes

1 Tbsp. prepared hot tomato salsa or
  2 jalapeños, seeded and chopped

1/4 cup stuffed green olives, sliced

1/2 tsp. cinnamon

1/2 tsp. ground cloves

salt and ground pepper, to taste

1 tart apple, peeled and chopped

METHOD

Sauté onion and garlic in the olive oil, add the ground beef, and cook to brown. Stir in remaining ingredients, except the apple. Bring to a boil, then reduce to a simmer, and cook for about 1/2 hour. Stir in the apple, cook for another 5 minutes, remove from heat, and set aside.

FOR THE TOPPING

2 large potatoes, peeled and chopped

2 sweet potatoes, peeled and chopped

1 Tbsp. unsalted butter

1/4 cup milk

salt and ground pepper, to taste

METHOD

Boil potatoes in salted water until tender, then drain and mash with butter, milk, salt, and pepper.

To assemble, spoon beef mixture into a 9-inch pie pan or 8- x 12-inch casserole dish and cover evenly with mashed potatoes, spreading with a spatula. Bake at 350° F for 30 to 45 minutes, until heated through. Serve with a green salad and salsa, homemade (see page 122) or store-bought or chili sauce.

Seafood "Annie Savoy"

At Grenville's, all of our pasta dishes were named after female movie characters. I have always been particularly fond of Susan Sarandon and consider her work in Bull Durham *to be most delectable. This rich and sassy dish was named after the crazy, sexy, wonderful romantic that she played. Seafood "Annie Savoy" is delicious over pasta, rolled in a flour tortilla, or as a crepe filling with a little reserved to use as a sauce on top.*

2 8 oz. salmon fillets

splash of white wine

peppercorns

12 large shrimp, peeled and deveined

1/4 cup unsalted butter

1 small onion, finely chopped

**2 pickled or fresh jalapeño peppers,
   seeded and finely diced**

1/4 cup all purpose flour

1/2 cup milk

1/2 cup Swiss cheese, grated

**2 bunches fresh spinach, steamed, strained,
   and chopped**

1/2 cup sour cream

METHOD

Poach the salmon in water to cover with a generous splash of white wine and a few peppercorns. Remove salmon using a slotted spoon and place in a bowl to cool. In the same liquid, poach the shrimp briefly, until pink and firm. Remove shrimp to the salmon bowl and strain the leftover seafood stock and reserve.

In a saucepan, melt the butter and sauté the onion and jalapeños until the onion is soft and transparent. Sprinkle in the flour and mix, then slowly drizzle in 1/2 cup of the reserved stock, stirring constantly. As the mixture begins to thicken, slowly add the milk and continue stirring. Stir in grated cheese until melted and remove from heat. Add chopped spinach and sour cream. Crumble salmon fillets into mixture, and then add whole shrimp.

Now you have a fantastic pasta sauce that can be tossed with fettuccine or baked with extra cheese in layers to make a seafood lasagna.

Spinach and Chevre Tart

1 prepared 9-inch pie crust
   (see Most-Trusted Pie Pastry, page 142)
1 bunch green onions, chopped
1/4 cup fresh herbs (any of basil, dill,
   parsley, etc.), chopped
1 Tbsp. unsalted butter
4 cups spinach, cleaned, stems removed
4 eggs
2 cups milk or 1 cup milk and 1 cup cream
pinch of dry mustard
pinch of nutmeg
salt and ground pepper, to taste
6 oz. softened goat cheese

METHOD

Sauté onions and herbs in butter until the onions are transparent. Add spinach leaves a little at a time until wilted, remove from heat and set aside. Whisk together eggs, milk, mustard, nutmeg, salt, pepper, and 1/2 of the goat cheese. Prick the prepared pie crust with a fork in several places. Spread spinach and onion mixture over the crust and crumble the remaining goat cheese on top. Pour on egg mixture and bake for 1 hour at 350° F, until firm. Let sit briefly, to set, before serving.

Spinach and Feta Strudel

This dish is a variation on the classic Greek spanakopita. Adding dilled mashed potatoes makes it smooth, more complex, and absolutely delicious.

FOR THE FILLING

4 medium potatoes, peeled and coarsely chopped

2 cloves garlic, peeled

1/2 cup buttermilk

ground black pepper, to taste

1 medium onion, finely chopped

1/4 cup fresh dill, chopped

1 Tbsp. unsalted butter

4 cups spinach, well cleaned

2 cups feta cheese, crumbled

METHOD

Boil potatoes in water with the garlic until potatoes are soft. Drain and mash potatoes and garlic with buttermilk and black pepper. Set aside. Sauté onions and dill in butter until onions are transparent, and add to potatoes. Steam spinach until wilted, then drain, pressing out excess moisture, then coarsely chop. Combine potato mixture, spinach, and feta in a large bowl.

TO ASSEMBLE

1 package phyllo pastry, defrosted

1/4 cup unsalted butter, melted

METHOD

Unwrap phyllo dough and separate one sheet. Lightly butter half the sheet and fold over widthwise once to form a long rectangle. Repeat with a second sheet so that there are four layers. Place two generous scoops of filling near the bottom of the pastry. Roll up from the bottom, folding over the sides to seal in the filling, and continue rolling to form a neat cylinder. Repeat to make six strudels. Brush with remainder of melted butter and bake on a cookie sheet at 350° F for 15 to 20 minutes. Strudels should be golden brown.

This dish can be made in advance, frozen, and then baked directly from the freezer. Tastes great with one of our Fruit Chutneys (see page 117-118) and a salsa of your choice.

Extra phyllo can be refrozen if tightly wrapped.

Jambalaya

FOR 4-6 PORTIONS

1 onion, chopped

2 cloves garlic, minced

1 Tbsp. olive oil

1 bell pepper, seeded and coarsely
chopped

1 fresh hot pepper, seeded and
diced (optional)

2 stalks celery, sliced

1/4 cup fresh parsley, chopped

1 28 oz. can of plum tomatoes, diced

1 tsp. oregano

Tabasco sauce, or prepared salsa, to taste

4 cups cooked chicken, shredded or
chopped

2 spicy sausages, pan-fried and sliced

1/2 lb. large raw shrimp, peeled and
deveined

salt and ground pepper, to taste

METHOD

In a large saucepan, sauté the onions
and garlic in olive oil until the onions are
transparent. Add the bell pepper, hot
pepper, celery, and parsley and cook
briefly. Add the tomatoes, oregano,
Tabasco, chicken, and sausage and simmer for 15 minutes. Finally, add the
shrimp and cook until they are pink and
firm, another 2 to 3 minutes. Taste and
season with more Tabasco or salsa. Serve
over rice or pasta.

MAIN COURSES

Food Fads

CHICKEN & GAME
Lucinda's Chicken
Stuffed Breast of Chicken with Spinach,
   Figs, and Prosciutto
Curried Chicken Pot Pie with Savoury
   Cornmeal Crust
Cornish Hens with Marmalade
   Merlot Glaze

BEEF
Beef Tenderloin with Gorgonzola and
   Caramelized Onions
Grenville's Drunken Rib-Eye Steak

LAMB
Lamb Shank Stew
Lamb Chops with Lemon Mint Butter

PORK
Pork Tenderloin Medallions with
   Blueberry Mustard Sauce
Pork Tenderloin with Goat Cheese and
   Mango Jalapeño Sauce

A Paramount Christmas

FISH & SEAFOOD
Fish Florentine with Portobello
   Mushrooms
Fillet of Arctic Char à la Grecque
Salmon Fillets—Two Ways
Seafood Stew "Romagna"

SHRIMP
A Shrimp Tale
Creole Shrimp
Curried Shrimp—Two Ways
Shrimp à la Grecque
Shrimp Provençale
Thai Shrimp

VEGETABLE
Potato, Chickpea, and Cauliflower Curry
La Strata—A Vegetable Strudel
Vegetable Tagine—A Moroccan-Inspired
   Stew
Gado Gado with Warm Peanut Sauce
Rustic Bean Stew

PASTA
Grenville's Pasta Bar
Basic Tomato Sauce and Variations
Olive Oil Sauces
Cream Sauces

Food Fads

I have never been of the opinion that food is an art form in its preparation or its service. No matter how beautiful the plate or exquisite the flavour, food endures only as long as it takes to consume it. Chefs and people who write about food can posture and exclaim, ad nauseam, but as far as I'm concerned, food is part of our basic experience and little more than a most pleasurable necessity.

As with all fashion, food trends are foisted on the public with little discussion. Unsuspecting diners enter a hip, new restaurant and are expected to adjust their expectations to suit the vision of the chef. The pricier the plate, the pushier the agenda. A veteran of the service industry almost throttled the diminutive chef at the now-deceased Parrot, in Toronto, for refusing to re-cook a rare duck breast that her elderly, Italian parent couldn't eat. "Who the hell does he think he is?" wailed Wanda. "We're paying a small fortune to show my folks a good time on their anniversary, and this little prince ruins the whole evening because somebody told him that duck is better bloody!"

I opened my first restaurant when "nouvelle cuisine" was the rage, and delicate cuts of meat were presented next to a fan of four or five snow peas, alongside turned carrots and potatoes the size of rabbit droppings. Needless to say, this was not a big hit in a small Ontario town. Customers were open to new flavours being offered but not the meagre portions. Spending most of my career in the hinterlands has kept both my cooking and ambition on an even keel. Catering to a clientele that knows what it likes, and insists on having it, has precipitated a tendency to bend to the whim of those who are paying the piper.

The Eighties! That's about the time when chefs started putting sauces underneath sliced main courses and then barely steaming the vegetables, so that their vibrant colours were maintained. As well, stark white plates were the fashion, and servers would present the meal as if it was worthy of a standing ovation. Pretty food? Certainly! Attractive servers? Without a doubt! But was it art? Certainly not for the person who had to clear the plate.

Popular recently, though showing no signs of wear, is the presentation of dinner as a skyscraper! Celebrity chefs have elevated the food architecturally in one way or another, and the result is actually quite charming, as long as you don't push down too hard on one part of your meal and send the rest careening across the room. Where once, one or two simple vegetables sufficed, the trend is to present a copious array of exotics, arranged dramatically. Plates are large, heavy, and brightly coloured, and the food looks sensational. So...where do we go from here?

On a short holiday weekend of dining in some of Toronto's finer establishments, I was alarmed to find the presence of actual building materials both descriptively on menus and as reality on plates. Cooking salmon on a piece of cedar may impart some flavour to the fish—but as an eating experience? Imagine skipping the formality of plates and dining directly on your picnic table. Chicken cooked under a brick sounds slightly sadistic to me. One would think that we abuse the poor birds enough while they're alive. Thankfully, the chef saw fit to keep the masonry in the kitchen and spared me the sound of knife grating against brick.

Another restaurant, the home of one of Canada's most famous chefs, served a simple goat cheese tart on a piece of a log. What could possibly be the motivation for this? We were in a museum, so perhaps, after the meal was eaten, Glenna was supposed to count the rings and guess the age of the tree that it was cut from. Our delightful waitress was dumbstruck when I queried her about the reason for putting a piece of wood on the plate. Poor thing. She had already done an excellent job fielding my somewhat sarcastic remark concerning the presence of butter (almost an extinct species as an accompaniment to bread) in a chic Toronto dining spot. She'd already smiled, rolled her eyes, and told us how the chef (she used his first name) "actually loves bread and butter," and that "his philosophy could be called 'traditional'...using familiar ingredients in new and exciting ways." I guess that explains the log.

CHICKEN & GAME

Lucinda's Chicken

Glenna worked for a pleasant year as a chef at an Ottawa catering company called Ryley and Maclaughlan. Cindy Ryley, one of the owners, was a huge fan of combining sun-dried tomatoes with goat cheese. Through the big picture window that fronted their lovely kitchen, Cindy, her partner Heather, and Glenna happily gabbed as they created meals for their posh government and foreign service clientele. Some dishes travel better through time than others, and Lucinda Ryley's chicken is, for us, a modern classic.

SERVES 4

4 chicken breasts, skinned and deboned

salt and ground pepper, to taste

2 Tbsp. unsalted butter

4 green onions, chopped

splash of white wine

1/4 cup sun-dried tomatoes, soaked in
    boiling water for about 20 minutes
    and chopped

4 oz. soft unripened goat cheese

1 1/2 cups whipping cream

METHOD

Rinse the chicken breasts, pat dry, sprinkle with salt and pepper, and brown both sides in a heavy skillet in half of the butter. Remove from heat to a baking sheet and place in the oven at 350° F. In the same skillet, add the rest of the butter and sauté green onions for about 2 minutes. Deglaze with a splash of white wine, add tomatoes, and crumble in goat cheese. Stir in heavy cream and a few twists of pepper. The sauce will begin to bubble and thicken and turn a pretty terra cotta colour. Remove cooked chicken breasts from the oven, place on plates, and smother with sauce.

Stuffed Breast of Chicken with Spinach, Figs, and Prosciutto

There are certain dishes that bring back memories, and this chicken dish is very evocative of our time in Ottawa. The process is more work than most, but if the flavours and ingredients appeal, then it's definitely worth the effort. I can summon up the taste simply from reading the recipe, which speaks of its strengths. It is certainly suitable if you want to make an impression.

4 chicken breasts, skinned and deboned

salt and ground pepper, to taste

1 bunch of spinach, stems removed

4 thin slices prosciutto

2 dried figs, chopped

1/4 cup toasted almonds, chopped

1/8 cup parmesan cheese, grated

3 Tbsp. unsalted butter

3 green onions, chopped, or 1-2 shallots, minced

1/2 cup mushrooms, any variety, thinly sliced

splash of dry Marsala wine

1/2 cup whipping cream

METHOD

Pound chicken breasts between two sheets of waxed paper until thin. Discard the paper. Season chicken with salt and pepper and layer each breast with spinach leaves, prosciutto, chopped figs, almonds, and Parmesan. Roll up chicken breasts tightly to make a package and place, seam down, on a plate lined with fresh wax paper. You may use toothpicks to secure the breasts, if you wish. Refrigerate for at least 1/2 hour.

In a heavy skillet, sear the rolled chicken breasts in 2 tablespoons of the butter until browned. Transfer to 350° F oven and bake for about 20 minutes.

Meanwhile, add the rest of the butter to the skillet and sauté the green onions or shallots and mushrooms with a few twists of pepper. Deglaze with a splash of dry Marsala wine, then add whipping cream, and boil to reduce until thick.

Remove cooked chicken breasts from oven, slice with a sharp knife into 1-inch rings and lay attractively on serving plates. Pour thickened sauce over stuffed breasts and serve.

Curried Chicken Pot Pie with Savoury Cornmeal Crust

Prepare 1 batch cornmeal pastry (page 75) and set aside.

FILLING

1 onion, finely chopped

1 carrot, diced

2 stalks celery, chopped

2 cloves garlic, minced

1 Tbsp. unsalted butter

dry white wine

2 Tbsp. curry powder

1 Tbsp. flour

1 cup milk

1 cup chicken stock

2 cups cooked chicken

1 Tbsp. chutney, store-bought or try Apple Plum Chutney (see page 118), or marmalade

1 handful frozen or fresh peas

salt and pepper, to taste

METHOD

In a medium saucepan, sauté onions, carrots, celery, and garlic in butter until onions are wilted and aromatic. Deglaze by adding a generous splash of white wine.

Lower the heat and stir in curry powder and flour, mixing thoroughly. Slowly add milk and stock, stirring with a wooden spoon until the mixture (roux) is thick. Add chicken, chutney, peas, salt, and pepper to taste, and continue cooking approximately 2 minutes longer.

Cut the pastry dough in two, making one half slightly larger than the other. Roll out each portion of pastry on a floured surface to 1/4-inch thickness. Line bottom of a pie plate with larger pastry to overlap the edges. Pour the creamy filling into the pastry, cover with remaining pastry and crimp the edges together. Slit the top so the steam can escape.

Bake at 350° F for 30 to 45 minutes until the top is golden brown. Serve with chutney and a crisp salad.

Cornmeal Pastry—
A savoury crust

MAKES 2 PIE CRUSTS

1 1/2 cups all-purpose flour

1/3 cup cornmeal

1/2 tsp. salt

1/4 cup unsalted butter, cut into
   small pieces

 3 Tbsp. cold shortening

1 egg

1/2 cup ice water (you may need more)

METHOD

With a pastry cutter or two knives, combine flour, cornmeal, salt, butter, and shortening until the mixture resembles coarse meal. Mix the egg and water together, sprinkle over mixture, and work the dough quickly by hand to form a ball. Use a bit more water if the mixture is too dry and doesn't hold together. Wrap and chill for at least 1/2 hour.

Cornish Hens with
Marmalade Merlot Glaze

SERVES 4, 1 HEN PER PERSON

1 cup Merlot wine

1/2 cup orange marmalade

2 tsp. curry powder

4 Cornish game hens, deboned if possible

olive oil

salt and ground pepper

4 sprigs fresh parsley, finely chopped

METHOD

To make the glaze, place Merlot and marmalade in a small saucepan, bring to a boil, and reduce to a syrup. Add curry powder and stir to dissolve. Set aside.

Rub the hens with olive oil and sprinkle with salt and ground pepper. Place in a baking pan and lightly spoon 1/3 of the sauce over. Bake at 350° F for 1/2 hour. Remove from oven and baste with 1/3 more of the glaze. Roast for 45 minutes longer. Place hens on serving plate and serve with remaining sauce. Sprinkle with chopped parsley.

BEEF

Beef Tenderloin with Gorgonzola and Caramelized Onions

SERVES 4

2 red or white onions, sliced in rings

1 Tbsp. unsalted butter

pinch of salt

ground black pepper, to taste

splash of balsamic vinegar

4 6 oz. pieces of beef tenderloin

4 oz. gorgonzola cheese, cut into 4 slices

METHOD

For the onions:

Melt the butter in a large, non-stick frying pan. Add the onions but do not stir. Let the onions cook over medium heat and shake the pan so that they don't stick. Continue cooking but not stirring, adding salt and pepper. When the onions have browned, stir, reduce heat and simmer for about 20 minutes, with a splash of balsamic vinegar and a bit of water if they appear too dry. Stir occasionally. When onions have stewed to the point where they are syrupy and mahogany coloured, remove from heat.

For the beef:

Make horizontal slits in the middle of each filet of beef and wedge in a piece of cheese. Broil for 3 minutes then turn and broil for 3 minutes longer. Steaks will be rare. Top with caramelized onions.

Grenville's Drunken Rib-Eye Steak

The first two cooks we hired at Grenville's were named Ross and Buzzo. I can't remember who was hired first, but they had worked together in some other incarnation and knew their way around a kitchen, as well as the Ottawa restaurant scene. They pegged us for the suckers we were, right off the bat.

When we purchased the lovely Victorian house on Somerset Street, it had already been turned into a restaurant called La Rose des Sables and was equipped with a sizable kitchen. One feature was a huge, 1000-pound charcoal barbecue that the previous owner had imported from Morocco. At our last restaurant, the grill had been a cast iron pan set on a gas burner, so this was truly going from the ridiculous to the sublime. Every two weeks, 144 big bags of charcoal were loaded into the cellar to fuel the monstrous grill.

In order to make it worth our while, we featured a variety of steaks and chops "grilled to perfection" on our menu. The kitchen boys recommended a meat purveyor they knew who would drive his truck to the back door and sell meats at a wholesale price. I used to marvel at the amount of steak we were selling and sang the praises of that incredible barbecue, despite the fumes I breathed in nightly for months.

As in many kitchens, the bloom was off "la rose," and both Buzzo and Ross left our employ within weeks of each other. Around this time, I noticed a sharp drop in the amount of rib eye and strip loin that we were purchasing from our travelling meat man. One day, I questioned him about this phenomenon, as sales didn't seem to have decreased. He smiled, shook his head, and was never seen again. Chris Grenville, one of our partners, commented that she'd always wondered what Buzzo was carrying in his overstuffed gym bag!

1 clove garlic, minced

2 tsp. white pepper

1/4 cup Hungarian paprika

2 Tbsp. dry mustard

2 Tbsp. Worcestershire sauce

1/2 cup beer

4 8 oz. rib-eye steaks

METHOD

In a bowl, combine all ingredients except steak to form a paste. Slather steaks with paste and barbecue or broil, 3 to 5 minutes per side for medium rare.

This steak tastes great with Mushroom Salsa (see page 120).

LAMB

Lamb Shank Stew

SERVES 4-6

Lamb shank lends itself well to stewing. The recipe that follows plays to its strong suit as a comfort food. For some, lamb is an exotic meat. It certainly is tasty and aromatic, and this presentation brings it home in a most unpretentious fashion. If this were made with cubed beef, I would call it Irish Stew.

4-6 lamb shanks

all-purpose flour, for dredging

4 Tbsp. olive oil

2 onions, chopped

3 potatoes, peeled and chopped

2 carrots, peeled and thickly sliced

2 parsnips, peeled and sliced

2 cloves garlic, minced

2 tsp. thyme

2 tsp. rosemary

water

salt and ground black pepper, to taste

Worcestershire sauce

METHOD

Dredge lamb shanks in flour and brown in half of the olive oil in a large pot. Remove and set aside. Add the rest of the oil and sauté the vegetables and herbs until onions begin to wilt. Add 3 to 4 cups of water and, using a wooden spoon, scrape up any flour that might stick to the bottom of the pot. Return shanks to the pot, sprinkle with salt and ground pepper and add a few splashes of Worcestershire sauce. Simmer for about an hour or cover and bake at 350° F for 45 minutes to an hour. Stir occasionally. Taste gravy and season accordingly. Serve shanks in a large pasta bowl surrounded by vegetables and sauce.

Lamb Chops with Lemon Mint Butter

SERVES 4 (2 CHOPS PER PERSON)

For 8 loin lamb chops:

THE MARINADE

3 Tbsp. lemon juice

1/2 tsp. salt

3 Tbsp. olive oil

1 Tbsp. mint leaves, chopped

ground pepper, to taste

METHOD

Combine ingredients and pour over chops in a shallow dish or baking pan. Marinate for at least an hour at room temperature, turning chops every 15 minutes. If marinating for a longer period, chops should be refrigerated.

FOR THE BUTTER

1/2 cup unsalted butter, softened

2 Tbsp. lemon juice

1 tsp. grated lemon rind

2 Tbsp. mint leaves, chopped

salt and pepper, to taste

METHOD

Blend all ingredients together in a bowl and place on a sheet of plastic wrap. Using the plastic wrap as an aid, form the herb butter into a log and refrigerate.

FOR THE LAMB

Place the marinated chops on a pan and broil under high heat for about 3 minutes per side. Remove to serving plates and top with 2 coin-sized rings of chilled butter per chop.

Serve with mashed potatoes or try Pecorino Potatoes (see page 112) and Steamed Green Vegetables (see page 110).

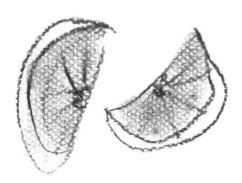

PORK

Pork Tenderloin Medallions with Blueberry Mustard Sauce

FOR 4 SERVINGS

2 lb. pork tenderloin, trimmed

METHOD

Cut tenderloin into 1/2-inch rounds. Place rounds between two pieces of waxed paper and pound, using a mallet, until flattened. Set aside.

FOR THE SAUCE

1 cup blueberries, fresh or frozen
2 Tbsp. Dijon mustard
1/2 cup fresh mint or basil
splash of balsamic vinegar
ground black pepper, to taste
pinch of salt
1/2 cup olive oil

METHOD

Purée the ingredients together in a food processor or whisk by hand and slowly drizzle in 1/2 cup olive oil until thickened. Transfer to a bowl or jar, as you will have more sauce than you need.

To cook the rounds or "medallions," coat the bottom of a heavy skillet with:

1 Tbsp. unsalted butter or olive oil

Brown the tenderloin for approximately 1 minute per side and place onto baking sheet (in the restaurant, we use a pizza pan). Spoon blueberry sauce liberally over pork and bake at 350° F for 5 to 10 minutes, depending on how well you like your pork cooked. Remove from baking dish to warmed plates. The sauce should be an exceptional colour.

This sauce works very well for fish like salmon, char, or halibut, especially if you add 1 tablespoon of mayonnaise to the mix.

Pork Tenderloin with Goat Cheese and Mango Jalapeño Sauce

SERVES 4

A food critic, when reviewing Grenville's on Somerset, described this dish as "gharrish!" Something about the gaudy clash of colours and flavours unsettled the writer's sensibilities. Not so the dining public, nor we who created the dish. Pork tenderloin is a most civilized meat, as it is flavourful, easy to handle, and very adaptable when combined with even the most imaginative of ingredients. The tenderloin was originally stuffed, but this layering method is simpler and has much the same effect. In fact, you get more of the delicious goat cheese this way!

2 lb. pork tenderloin, trimmed and cut into 1/2-inch rounds

2 Tbsp. unsalted butter

1/2 lb. softened goat cheese

METHOD

Place rounds of pork between two pieces of waxed paper and gently pound into medallions. Set aside.

In a frying pan, brown the pork medallions in melted butter about 2 minutes per side and remove to a baking sheet. Using approximately 4 medallions per serving, layer pork and 1 tablespoon goat cheese, then pork, then goat cheese on the sheet, so that each portion has the 4 medallions separated by 3 tablespoons of cheese. Bake the pork and cheese on a baking sheet at 350° F for 5 to 7 minutes, until medallions have cooked through.

To serve, place a pool of mango sauce on each plate. Using a spatula, lift an entire serving of pork and cheese and place on top of sauce. Repeat for each serving. You may warm if you wish, but it works well at room temperature.

MANGO JALAPEÑO SAUCE

1 ripe mango, peeled and cut from the pit

2 jalapeño peppers, seeded and finely chopped (or leave the seeds in for extra heat)

1 cup orange juice

1/2 cup dark rum

a few leaves of fresh basil, chopped

METHOD

To make the sauce, purée 3/4 of the mango (reserving 1/4 of the flesh to chop by hand) with the jalapeños, orange juice, and rum in a food processor. Remove to a bowl and add some chopped mango pieces and the basil.

A Paramount Christmas

Having faced and survived the trauma of bankruptcy, I began to feel that nothing good would ever come out of our time spent in Ottawa. Both Glenna and I had good jobs, she in catering, I at a conference centre, with little of the stress that was implicit with owning a restaurant, but concern for our financial future was always foremost in my thoughts. Our daughters were both safely away at university, beginning their long relationship with the student loans department, and there was, despite some very good friends, little reason to stay in the city.

As Guelph had always been kind to us, and our ties to the community were still strong, I felt a tug (that was not shared by Glenna) to return and see what opportunities might make themselves available. During our absence, an old downtown hotel that had gone a familiar small-town route from family gathering and entertainment spot to home of strippers and bikers, had been sold, renovated, and needed someone to take ownership of the spacious restaurant and run the catering department for three function rooms. I met with the owner, who knew of our reputation and, within weeks, we packed up, moved into a tiny coach house, and opened The Paramount Café.

With the exception of having to serve a hotel breakfast (a nightmare if you've ever done it), running the restaurant was fairly routine. Loyal customers were eager to come back and partake of our hospitality and, aside from knocking heads with the hotel owner from time to time, things seemed promising.

Hotel dining rooms stay open 365 days a year. As restaurant owners, we expected to work most of the time, but Christmas, even for non-Christians, is treasured as a time to stay home and cuddle with family. The girls were coming home for the holidays and as they needed extra money, we decided that the four of us, plus Kael's best friend, Jessica Johnston, would serve Christmas dinner ourselves.

We had a young chef working for us at the time who was a wizard at deboning turkeys. As the reservation list started to grow, he set to work on preparing the birds that I would serve along with stuffing, vegetables, and gravy to the families that chose to dine out on December 25th. Understandably, none of our staff wanted to work, and so, confident that the family could manage, we gave everyone the day off.

By the time Christmas day finally arrived, there were more than 180 reservations. At $20 a head, we figured to make a pretty good buck. In a moment of macho insanity, I decided to handle the kitchen by myself, with Glenna and the girls working the floor.

The kitchen at the hotel was very well equipped and had a big steam table that we never used. It could be filled up with prepared foods to keep them hot for hours. We had never served food this way, as freshness was our hallmark, and we considered cafeteria-style cooking methods to be beneath us. Under these circumstances, our principles were thrown to the wind as we needed all the help technology could give us.

The first sitting ran as smoothly as clockwork. We were fresh, like the vegetables that started out in the steam table, but as the hours wore on, we began to wilt at about the same rate. Certain groups of holiday customers do very little dining out at other times of the year. As a result, they can be rather high maintenance. Add to that the likelihood that some of them would rather be anywhere but with their families, and you might have some idea of what the room was like to serve. Glenna had plenty of experience dealing with the stresses of waiting tables, but our daughters, who did not consider service to be particularly appealing, started bitching early on, sarcastically expressing their desire to kill some of the customers or walk out altogether. Jessica, a complete newcomer to life in the restaurant trenches, went into shock, hid in the office and chain-smoked until it was over.

By 8:30, just about everyone was fed and gone and I thought I might die right there on the cutting board. When I turned around to look at the state of the kitchen, the reality that there was no one to clean up hit me like a ton of bricks and I crumpled to the floor in a pool of tears. Well ... not quite.

Luckily, a friend of the girls' arrived, and I bribed him with cash to do the dishes. The thousands of dollars we took in and divided up did little to ease the cloud of self-pity that hung over us on a day when it seemed that everyone but us was entitled to a good time.

The hotel fell on bad financial times, and by the time Yuletide rolled around again, we were working at The Bookshelf and spending Christmas day at home, together in front of the fire.

FISH & SEAFOOD

Fish Florentine with Portobello Mushrooms

SERVES 4

This dish is traditionally prepared with sole, but any nice white fish will do.

1 onion, diced

1 Tbsp. unsalted butter

3 portobello mushrooms, sliced

splash of white wine

4 cups spinach leaves, cleaned

salt and ground pepper, to taste

pinch of cayenne

1/4 cup whipping cream

2 lb. fish fillets

juice of 1/2 lemon

METHOD

In a frying pan, sauté onions in the butter until wilted. Add the sliced mushrooms and continue cooking until they are soft. Deglaze with a splash of white wine and add the spinach, which will cook quickly. Add salt and ground pepper to taste, a pinch of cayenne, and the cream. Cook until the cream has reduced but isn't too thick.

Place the fish fillets in a baking dish and sprinkle with lemon juice. Spoon over spinach and mushroom sauce and bake at 350° F for 30 minutes.

Serve with broad egg noodles cooked and sautéed in 2 tablespoons olive oil in a non-stick pan. Sprinkle generously with salt, pepper, and parmesan.

Fillet of Arctic Char à la Grecque

SERVES 4

4 6-8 oz. arctic char fillets, or firm-fleshed
   fish

salt and ground black pepper, to taste

1 large sweet red pepper, seeded
   and diced

1 ripe tomato, seeded and diced

1 shallot, minced

12 kalamata olives, pitted and chopped

1/4 cup fresh basil leaves, chopped or
   1 tsp. dry basil

1/4 cup feta cheese, finely crumbled

pinch of salt

juice of 1 lemon

1 Tbsp. olive oil

METHOD

Place char fillets on a baking sheet and
season lightly with salt and ground
pepper. Place chopped red pepper and
tomato in a bowl and mix with the other
ingredients. Spoon mixture over fish
fillets and bake at 350° F for 15 minutes.

*If using fish thicker than char (e.g.,
salmon or halibut), bake fish for 10 minutes with just a sprinkle of olive oil, salt,
and pepper and then spoon on the topping and bake for another 10 to 15 minutes until fish is cooked through. If you
wish to add another dimension to the
dish, dredge the fillets in cornmeal
before baking.*

Salmon Fillets—Two Ways

Salmon Fillets with Asian Marinade

SERVES 4

You will need 4 6-8oz. salmon fillets and either a broiler set on high or a 350° F oven if you would rather bake the fish.

MARINADE

3 cloves garlic, minced

1 Tbsp. fresh grated ginger

1/2 cup soy sauce

1/2 cup orange juice

1/2 cup dry sherry

3 Tbsp. granulated sugar

METHOD

Mix all ingredients together in a bowl, dissolving the sugar. Pour over salmon fillets, preferably in a glass baking pan or bowl, and refrigerate for at least 2 hours.

To cook, remove fish from marinade, set on broiling pan and place under broiler for at least 5 minutes until fillet is firm, or bake at 350° F for 15 minutes. Spoon additional marinade over fish halfway through baking process or just before serving, if using a broiler. Serve immediately atop Stir-fry Rice Noodles (see page 115). Sprinkle with chopped green onions and toasted sesame seeds.

Salmon Fillets with Mint-Mustard Sauce

SERVES 4

The combination of mint, mustard, and salmon is extremely satisfying. Adding a tablespoon of mayonnaise to the mustard will make it richer and more mellow.

METHOD

Pat dry 4 6-8 oz. salmon fillets and place in a lightly greased baking pan. Squeeze the juice of 1/2 lemon over the fish and set aside. Preheat oven to 350° F.

SAUCE

3 Tbsp. Dijon mustard

3 Tbsp. grain mustard

3 Tbsp. white wine vinegar

1/2 cup firmly packed mint leaves

1 Tbsp. mayonnaise (optional)

1 1/2 cups olive oil

In a food processor, blend the mustard, vinegar, mint, and mayonnaise. Drizzle in the olive oil to emulsify. Lightly spoon the sauce over fillets and bake for about 15 minutes. Spoon on additional sauce and bake another 5 minutes until salmon is firm.

Seafood Stew "Romagna"

Cooking the onions in vinegar, crushing the tomatoes on the side of the pot and pushing, not stirring, the fish is a technique found in traditional Northern Italian cuisine.

2 large onions, chopped

1 anchovy fillet, rinsed and finely chopped

1/4 cup red wine vinegar

3 cloves garlic, minced

2 1- x 2-inch strips of lemon peel, white pith removed

28 oz. canned whole tomatoes

5 Tbsp. olive oil

2 cups dry white wine

2 cups fish stock, or water

salt and ground pepper

1/4 cup Italian parsley, chopped

2 lb. firm-fleshed white fish, chopped in chunks

METHOD

Sweat the onions, anchovy, and vinegar in a large, covered Dutch oven, or in a soup pot, on medium-high heat for 5 minutes. The liquid will reduce considerably, and the anchovies will disintegrate. Stir in garlic, lemon peel, and tomatoes with their juice and crush the tomatoes with a wooden spoon against the side of the pot so they remain chunky. Add the olive oil, wine, and stock or water and season with salt and a generous amount of ground black pepper. Simmer for about an hour until thick and aromatic. Add the parsley and the fish and cook for 7 minutes until done. Push the fish around, rather than stirring. This stew can be prepared in advance without the fish and reheated, as long as you add the fish just before you're ready to serve. Remove lemon peel and discard. Serve with crusty Italian loaf or garlic bread and a crisp green salad.

Fish stews are always wonderful topped with aioli. A simple preparation is to crush 1 clove of garlic and coarse salt and mix it with the juice of one lemon, a cup of mayonnaise, and ground pepper.

SHRIMP

A Shrimp Tale

When I was growing up, dining out with my family was a Sunday evening ritual. Whether we were living in New York, Toronto, or Montreal, my parents favoured a select number of restaurants, and the five of us would pile into that year's Oldsmobile and head downtown to whichever familiar venue my father had selected. Chomping on a smelly stogie, my father, a big, broad-shouldered guy, would barrel into the joint and demand his table and favourite waitress. Not too many people said "no" to Jack and I remember cringing in the background as he peeled bills off a wad of cash to tip the maître d'.

My father always wanted us to appreciate the advantages we had, especially where food was concerned. When at home, if my mother served a meal that didn't appeal, he would quickly remind us that Gus and Mickey who lived next door were probably eating hot dogs and beans, and we should be grateful for the bounty before us. The son of immigrants, he considered food to be a sign of wealth and our refrigerators (there were two) were always filled to bursting with the food that he bought on a daily basis. Grocery shopping, like betting the ponies, was one of Jack's favourite pastimes and, though he kicked the gambling habit, he was a major shopper to his dying days.

When eating out, there were definitely certain items on the menu that were off limits as far as we children were concerned. I remember longing for the random treats that my father arbitrarily forbade. For some reason, asking for a Coke was considered a crime against humanity. The one dish that I craved more than any other was Shrimp Cocktail. But even saying the words angered my father, who was appalled that "these Hogtown hicks had the goddamned nerve to charge $3.50 for five crummy shrimp ... I used to take your mother to a swanky place in Brooklyn, where for three bucks, they gave you enough shrimp to feed an army!"

All I wanted was one of those stainless steel pedestals, filled with crushed ice, chopped lettuce, a pool of ruby red sauce, and those five, cold, curled, lovely pink bodies wrapped around the edges. Alas, it was not to be.

Years later, I am still fascinated by people's attitudes towards shrimp. No longer as exotic and expensive as in the days of my youth, shrimp can still have an odd effect on the public. Carrying a tray at a cocktail party, I've been mugged by greedy guests, crazed at the sight of free shrimp. It's as if everyone shared my early childhood denial and now lusts after something once forbidden.

Glenna and I both think that shrimp is one of the most adaptable and enjoyable foods on which to base a meal. We recommend that you purchase frozen, deveined, shell-on shrimp. 21/25 (the number of shrimp per pound) is a good size that is available from most purveyors. The shrimp can be thawed in the refrigerator during the day or are fine soaked briefly in water in order to remove the shells. Remember that shrimp cook very quickly and, if overdone, are hardly worth the effort.

Creole Shrimp

SERVES 4

2 cloves garlic, minced

1 onion, coarsely chopped

3 stalks celery, sliced

1 green pepper, seeded and coarsely
  chopped

1 sweet red pepper, coarsely chopped

1 fresh jalapeño pepper, seeded and
  chopped

1 Tbsp. olive oil

1 tsp. dried basil

1 tsp. dried thyme

3 cups Roma tomatoes, chopped

juice of 1 lemon

pinch of brown sugar

Tabasco sauce, to taste

salt and ground pepper, to taste

1 lb. shrimp, peeled and deveined

METHOD

In a saucepan, sauté garlic, onions, celery, and peppers in olive oil until the vegetables begin to soften, remembering that crunchiness makes this dish distinctive. Stir in the herbs and add tomatoes, lemon juice, sugar, Tabasco, salt, and ground pepper. Let the tomatoes stew for 5 to 10 minutes, add the shrimp, and cook until they are pink and firm. Serve immediately on steamed long grain white rice.

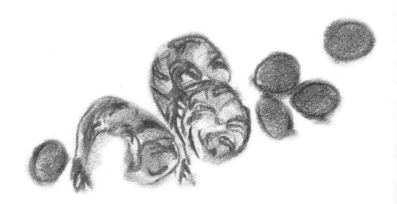

Curried Shrimp—Two Ways

The following recipes will serve 4 people. They are extremely quick to make and are excellent served over rice, pasta, or with any grain you fancy.

Curried Shrimp #1

1 clove garlic, minced

1 small onion, diced

2 stalks celery, diced

1 Tbsp. unsalted butter or olive oil

1-2 Tbsp. curry powder

1 Tbsp. chili powder

1 28 oz. can diced plum tomatoes

1 heaping Tbsp. chutney, homemade or
    store-bought, or marmalade

1 lb. shrimp, peeled and deveined

METHOD

Sauté garlic, onions, and celery in butter or olive oil in a large skillet until soft. Stir in the spices and tomatoes and simmer for 10 minutes. Add the chutney and stir to incorporate. Taste and adjust seasoning to suit. Add the shrimp and cook until pink and firm. Serve immediately. This is great over basmati rice.

Curried Shrimp #2

1 clove garlic, minced

1 Tbsp. fresh ginger, minced

4 green onions, chopped

8 white mushrooms, sliced

1 Tbsp. unsalted butter or olive oil

splash of dry white wine

1-2 Tbsp. curry powder

1-2 Tbsp. tomato salsa

1 lb. shrimp, peeled and deveined

1/2 cup whipping cream

METHOD

In a heavy skillet, briefly sauté garlic, ginger, onions, and mushrooms in the butter. Deglaze by adding a splash of white wine, turn down the heat and add curry powder and salsa. Add shrimp and stir to mix well, then add whipping cream and let bubble until thick, creamy, and colourful. Serve tossed with thin rice noodles, Chinese egg noodles, or basmati rice.

Serve with Cucumber Raita (see page 124 and top with toasted almonds and currants.

Shrimp à la Grecque

This dish is so easy and delicious that it's almost criminal.

SERVES 4

4 cups Basic Tomato Sauce (see page 102)

1/4 cup dry white wine

1 cup feta cheese, crumbled

1 Tbsp. dried oregano

ground black pepper, to taste

6 black olives, pitted and halved (optional)

1 lb. shrimp, peeled and deveined

METHOD

Heat the tomato sauce in a saucepan, add the white wine, crumbled feta, oregano, pepper, and optional black olives. Stir to incorporate, and cook until the sauce is bubbling. Add the shrimp and simmer until pink and firm. Serve immediately on white rice, couscous, or orzo.

Shrimp Provençale

This is an excellent dish for an impromptu dinner party.

SERVES 4

4 cloves garlic, minced

1 small red onion, finely diced

1/4 cup olive oil

splash of dry white wine

1 sweet red pepper, seeded and chopped

1 green pepper, seeded and chopped

15 cherry tomatoes, cut in half

15 black olives, pitted and coarsely
  chopped

1 lb. shrimp, peeled and deveined

ground black pepper, to taste

2 Tbsp. dried oregano

1/4 cup parmesan, grated

METHOD

In a large skillet, sauté garlic and red onions in olive oil. Deglaze by adding a splash of white wine, then add sweet peppers, cherry tomatoes, and olives and continue cooking, stirring constantly until tomatoes begin to release their juice. Add shrimp, black pepper, and oregano and toss together with half of the parmesan as shrimp begin to cook and get firm. Serve immediately and top with the rest of the cheese.

It's perfect with cheese-filled tortellini.

Thai Shrimp

A truly delicious meal with the unique Thai-inspired combination of lemon grass, ginger, and coconut milk.

SERVES 4

3 cloves garlic, minced

1 Tbsp. fresh ginger, minced

1/2 bunch green onions, chopped

1 stalk lemon grass, tender part,
finely chopped

1 Tbsp. sesame oil

1 large sweet red pepper, seeded and
cut in chunks

1/2 tsp. turmeric

1/4 tsp. hot pepper flakes

splash of soy sauce

juice of 2 limes

1/4 cup fresh coriander, chopped

1 cup canned coconut milk

1 lb. shrimp, peeled and deveined

toasted sesame seeds

METHOD

In a wok, sauté garlic, ginger, onions, and lemon grass in sesame oil until aromatic. Add the red peppers and cook until they begin to soften. Stir in turmeric, hot pepper flakes, soy sauce, lime juice, coriander, and coconut milk and continue cooking about 5 minutes longer. Add the shrimp and toss until pink and firm. Sprinkle with toasted sesame seeds and more chopped green onions. Serve on basmati rice or tossed with rice noodles, or Chinese egg noodles.

VEGETABLE

Potato, Chickpea, and Cauliflower Curry

4 Tbsp. olive oil

1 medium onion, diced

1-inch piece fresh ginger, grated

2 Tbsp. dried cumin

3 Tbsp. mustard seeds

2 tsp. turmeric

2 tsp. salt

hot pepper flakes

6 medium potatoes, scrubbed and diced

1/4-1/2 cup water

1 medium head cauliflower, in florets

2 cups chickpeas, cooked or canned

1/2 cup fresh mint or coriander

 juice of 1 lemon

diced sweet red peppers for garnish

2 green onions, chopped

METHOD

Heat oil in a heavy pot. Add onion, ginger, and seasonings. Sauté until onions are soft and spices are integrated. Add the potatoes to the onions, stirring constantly to incorporate the seasonings and prevent sticking. Reduce the heat to medium and add 1/4 cup water. Cover the pot, stirring occasionally, adding more water gradually if needed. When the potatoes are tender-crisp, add the cauliflower and the chickpeas. Cover the pot and cook, stirring occasionally, until the vegetables are soft but not mushy. Add fresh mint or coriander and the lemon juice. Garnish with the red pepper and green onions for colour and crunch.

La Strata—A Vegetable Strudel

To make enough filling for six strudels:

1 onion, chopped

2 cups mushrooms, sliced

1 sweet red pepper, roasted, peeled, seeded, and chopped

4 large leeks, well cleaned and sliced thin (white part)

2 Tbsp. olive oil

1 tsp. dried oregano

1 tsp. dried thyme

1 tsp. dried tarragon

pinch of cayenne pepper

ground black pepper, to taste

juice and zest of 1 lemon

4 tomatoes, chopped

1 bunch spinach, cleaned and chopped

1/2 lb. feta cheese, crumbled

2 cups mozzarella or 1 1/2 cups Oka cheese, grated

METHOD

Sauté onions, mushrooms, red pepper, and leeks in oil in a large frying pan until leeks begin to soften and onions are wilted. Add seasonings, lemon juice, and zest and continue cooking until well blended. Add tomatoes and spinach and cook 5 minutes longer. Remove from heat and place ingredients into a colander to strain excess liquid. Put in a bowl and stir in feta and mozzarella.

TO ASSEMBLE

1 package phyllo pastry

1/4 cup unsalted butter, melted

Unwrap phyllo dough and separate one sheet. Lightly butter half the sheet and fold widthwise over once to form a long rectangle. Repeat with a second sheet so that there are four layers. Place two generous scoops of filling near the bottom of the pastry. Roll up from the bottom, folding over the sides to seal in the filling and continue folding to form a neat roll. Repeat to make six strudels, brush with remainder of melted butter, and bake on cookie sheet at 350° F for 15 to 20 minutes. Strudels should be golden brown. Tightly wrap remaining phyllo pastry and freeze.

The optional Oka cheese adds even more flavour to this delicious strudel.

Vegetable Tagine—A Moroccan-Inspired Stew

SERVES 6-8

2 onions, 1 coarsely chopped, 1 diced

2 Tbsp. olive oil

1 tsp. turmeric

1 tsp. cumin

1 tsp. ground coriander

1 tsp. paprika

pinch of cayenne

pinch of cinnamon

3 cloves garlic, minced

1 large potato, peeled and cut in chunks

1 sweet potato, peeled and cut in chunks

1 large carrot, peeled and cut in thick slices

1 sweet red pepper, seeded and chopped

1 squash (butternut or acorn), peeled and
   cut in chunks

1 small cauliflower, florets only

1 eggplant, peeled and coarsely chopped
   (optional)

water

1 handful raisins, apricots, or prunes,
   chopped

1/4 cup honey

1 28 oz. can diced tomatoes (juice included)

splash of hot pepper sauce

2 cups canned chickpeas, rinsed and
   drained

1 zucchini, coarsely chopped

juice of one lemon

salt and pepper

METHOD

In a large pot or Dutch oven, sauté the coarsely chopped onions in olive oil with the spices. Add the garlic and cook for about 5 minutes. Add the remaining vegetables, except zucchini and tomatoes, and continue to sauté until well coated. Add enough water to cover and simmer for 30 minutes. Meanwhile, in a medium pan, sauté the diced onion in a splash of olive oil with the raisins, apricots, or prunes, honey, tomatoes, and hot pepper sauce. Allow to thicken, stirring occasionally, then add to the simmering stew along with the chickpeas, zucchini, lemon juice, salt, and ground pepper to taste. Continue cooking for 15 minutes until vegetables are soft but not mushy, and serve. This dish is fine by itself or can be served on rice, couscous, or polenta.

Chopping the vegetables in various shapes and sizes makes a pleasing presentation.

Gado Gado—An Indonesian Salad with Warm Peanut Sauce

FOR 4 SALADS

6 new potatoes, quartered

1 1/2 cups green beans

1 small cauliflower, in florets

1 carrot, julienned

1 head lettuce, Boston or leaf

1/2 English cucumber, sliced

4 eggs, hardboiled, quartered

1/2 cup firm tofu (optional)

1 cup mung bean sprouts

handful toasted peanuts

METHOD

Boil potatoes until cooked, yet firm. Drain and set aside. Blanch green beans, cauliflower, and carrot until tender crisp. Plunge into ice water to maintain colour and texture. Tear lettuce and divide equally between four dinner plates. Distribute cucumber slices and the cooked vegetables, eggs, and tofu. Cover with warm peanut sauce and top generously with sprouts and toasted peanuts.

WARM PEANUT SAUCE

4 cloves garlic, chopped

2 Tbsp. ginger, chopped

1/2 cup coriander leaves

1/4 tsp. cayenne

splash canola oil

1 tsp. sesame oil

1 cup canned coconut milk

1 cup water

1 cup unsweetened peanut butter

1/2 Tbsp. soy sauce

1 Tbsp. brown sugar

2 Tbsp. lime juice

METHOD

Process garlic, ginger, coriander, cayenne and canola oil in a food processor to make a paste. In a small pot combine sesame oil, coconut milk, and water over medium heat. Stir in the prepared paste. Whisk in, a bit at a time, the peanut butter. Add the soy sauce, brown sugar, and lime juice. Stir for 5 minutes until well blended, thick, and smooth.

This peanut sauce is very versatile and keeps well. Use as a dipping sauce, toss with noodles (hot or cold), or stir in soups or stews that need a South Asian boost.

Rustic Bean Stew

4 Tbsp. olive oil

2 cups carrots, sliced

1 large onion, chopped

2 cloves garlic, minced

1 tsp. dry mustard

1 Tbsp. dried tarragon

1 tsp. dried thyme

1/2 tsp. cayenne pepper

2 sweet peppers (red, yellow, or both),
    seeded and coarsely chopped

2 cups mushrooms, quartered

3 tomatoes, chopped

1/2 small fennel bulb, sliced

1 potato, coarsely chopped

1/2-1 cup vegetable stock, liquid from
    beans or water

2 cups spinach or Swiss chard leaves,
    cleaned

3 cups beans, kidney beans, white beans,
    chickpeas, canned or dried and cooked

METHOD

In a large pot with a lid, heat the olive oil. Cook the carrots and onions, covered, on medium-high heat for 5 minutes. Add garlic and seasonings, including dry mustard, and cook for another 5 minutes. Reduce heat and add peppers, mushrooms, tomatoes, fennel, and potato, with water or stock. Stir to combine. Cover and simmer until the vegetables are tender-crisp. Add the greens, then the beans, and cook until the stew is hot. Serve with crusty bread, rice, or polenta.

Substitute or add any vegetables to the stew, alter the seasonings, but always include the dry mustard and cook with the pot covered.

PASTA

Grenville's Pasta Bar

I'll never know whether it was a mid-life crisis, or just plain insanity, but in 1987, I decided that it was time to sell The Baker St. Bistro and leave Guelph. By this time, we owned a second restaurant called Timer's, named after our 16-year-old cat, and though it struggled to make a buck, it certainly added to our resources. Our home, a century-old cottage that we had bought for $40,000, had more than tripled in value. The Bistro was a hot property, so with good friends as partners, and a sizable chunk of change, we decided to tackle the big city.

We went to Ottawa with the optimism nurtured by 10 successful years in a small town. Sadly, the free-spending Eighties that had been so kind to us were drawing to a close, and attitudes were changing like politics. Bankers in the capital considered restauranteurs to be a bad risk, so despite a considerable down payment, mortgage money was not forthcoming for the Victorian brownstone that we had found on trendy Somerset Street. I felt like a country bumpkin when the real estate agent brought us to a mortgage broker who was willing to finance the building, but who demanded thousands of dollars up front and an obscene mortgage rate to boot. Eager to begin, we foolishly took the deal.

After being in existence for about a year, Grenville's on Somerset began to hit its stride and become a popular dining spot. Glowing reviews from local critics certainly helped to establish our reputation in a cold city where we knew absolutely no one. Slow early sales had depleted our resources, so we were understandably relieved to see Grenville's star climbing on the horizon.

Not wanting to let any grass grow under our feet, we decided to renovate the second floor of the building and turn it into a Pasta Bar. Fortunately for us, a wonderful chef named Fraser Prince had found his way into our kitchen and was to spearhead the menu of our new folly. Fraser, currently the owner of the popular Arlequin in Toronto, was and is a great cook. We are friends to this day, and Glenna has always considered him her greatest inspiration when faced with the daily rigors of creating the countless sauces required to cover the ever-popular noodle.

Despite an incredible space designed by our partner Mark Grenville (now sadly deceased) and Fraser's exciting menu, the Pasta Bar never flew, and Grenville's eventually collapsed under the weight of all its debts.

Though the years have passed, and we've moved on from Grenville's, pasta sauces continue to be one of the staples of our menu. Glenna still enjoys creating new specials daily and many of the quick recipes that follow were first introduced to us by Fraser. Serve any of the sauces that follow with the pasta of your choice, from spaghetti to penne, a salad, some crusty bread, and a bottle of your favourite vino.

Basic Tomato Sauce and Variations

The most important thing to remember when making tomato sauce is to use the best quality ingredients available.

1 large onion, finely chopped

3 cloves garlic, minced

pinch of hot red pepper flakes

1 tsp. oregano or basil

salt and ground pepper, to taste

1/4 cup olive oil

1 28 oz. can of puréed Italian plum
    tomatoes

1 Tbsp. tomato paste

1 tsp. brown sugar

METHOD

Sauté onions, garlic, hot pepper flakes, and spices in olive oil until onions have softened. Stir in tomatoes, tomato paste, and brown sugar and bring to a boil. Lower heat and simmer until the sauce has reduced in volume and thickened approximately 1/2 hour. Taste and adjust seasoning.

VARIATIONS

With Wine

Add a generous splash of dry red or white wine and cook briefly before adding tomatoes. The flavour will become more robust.

With Mushrooms

Add 4 cups sliced mushrooms when sautéing onions.

Sauce Rosé

Add 1/4 cup whipping cream to simmering sauce.

With Chevre

Add 1/4-1/2 cup softened goat cheese and stir into simmering sauce just before serving.

With Roasted Red Peppers

Add 1 roasted sweet red pepper, skin and seeds removed, chopped.

Smoky

Sauté 4 strips of bacon, chopped, in a pan until crisp. Remove bacon from the pan and drain on paper towel. Pour off excess fat from the pan and deglaze with a splash of red wine, add tomato sauce, return bacon to the sauce, and heat through.

Norma

Sauté 1 small, firm eggplant, peeled and cubed, in olive oil to brown. Remove from the pan and drain on paper towel. Deglaze with a splash of red or white wine, and add tomato sauce and the eggplant. Simmer to heat through.

Stove-Top Lasagna

When the sauce is hot, add grated mozzarella cheese and cook without stirring until the cheese begins to bubble. Spoon sauce over prepared noodles, like fettuccine, and top with grated parmesan. Stir in a dollop of ricotta cheese for an even richer sauce.

With Sausage

Boil or grill 1 or 2 Italian sausages, slice, and add to simmering sauce.

À la Grecque

Crumble in 1/2-1 cup feta cheese, 12 pitted black olives, and extra oregano.

Puttanesca

Add 12 pitted olives, chopped, 1 tablespoon capers, drained, and 2 anchovy fillets, drained and chopped.

With Pesto

Add 2 Tbsp. John's Basil Pesto (see page 116) to simmering sauce.

Seafood Marinara

Add 6 to 9 whole shrimp, shelled and deveined, 12 cleaned fresh mussels, and 1/2 lb. white-fleshed fish, chopped, and some dry white wine. Simmer until shrimp turn pink and mussels have opened.

The addition of fresh chopped flat-leaf or Italian parsley adds another dimension, in both colour and flavour, to all tomato and other pasta sauce. Also, be sure to pass grated parmesan and hot pepper flakes.

Olive Oil Sauces

The quality of the olive oil used once again depends on the cook. The variety of flavours imparted by different oils is quite remarkable, and each dish will taste very much like the oil. The same holds true for cheese. Choose the best parmesan you can afford. We recommend Parmigiano-Reggiano. It has a rich, nutty taste and should be grated fresh.

Provençale

3 cloves garlic, minced

1/4 cup extra-virgin olive oil

1 small red onion, diced

1 sweet red or green pepper, seeded and chopped

12 cherry tomatoes, halved

6 kalamata olives, pitted and chopped

1 Tbsp. oregano

1/4 cup parmesan

METHOD

Sauté the garlic in olive oil. Add the remaining ingredients (except parmesan) and cook until the cherry tomatoes break down, creating the liquid of the sauce. Add cooked pasta to the pan with 1/4 cup grated parmesan. Stir to incorporate all the ingredients. Top with more cheese when serving. Great with cheese tortellini, ravioli, or rotini.

With Rapini and Olives

2 cloves garlic, minced

1 small onion, diced

1/4 cup olive oil

2 cups mushrooms, sliced

splash of white wine

florets from 1 bunch of rapini, steamed

1 bunch fresh basil, chopped

12 black or green olives, pitted and chopped

1/4 grated Asiago or pecorino cheese

METHOD

Sauté the garlic and onions in olive oil. Add the mushrooms and cook for 3 minutes. Deglaze the pan with white wine. Add the rapini, basil, and olives. Add cooked pasta and stir briefly until heated through. Stir in cheese and serve. Try fusilli or penne with this sauce.

Primavera

1 garlic clove, minced

1/2 cup each of carrots, zucchini, red,
   green, and yellow peppers, julienned

1/4 cup corn kernels

3 green onions, chopped

1/4 cup fresh or frozen peas

1/2 cup broccoli florets

1/4 cup olive oil

1/4 cup white wine

salt and pepper, to taste

chopped fresh herbs such as parsley,
   basil, or thyme

METHOD

Sauté the vegetables (use any other
vegetables that appeal) in olive oil until
tender-crisp. Add wine and season with
salt and pepper. Toss with cooked pasta
like spaghetti or linguine and toss with
fresh herbs and grated parmesan.

With Leeks and Sausage

1 leek, white part, cleaned and thinly sliced

1/4 cup olive oil

1-2 cloves garlic, minced

2 cups mushrooms, sliced

1 sweet red pepper, roasted, seeded,
   peeled, and chopped

6 kalamata olives, pitted and chopped

1 spicy Italian sausage, boiled and sliced

1/4 cup chicken stock or white wine or
   some stock from cooking the sausage

pinch of hot red pepper flakes

1 tsp. oregano or basil

METHOD

Sauté leeks in olive oil. Add garlic, mushrooms, roasted pepper, and olives. Add
sausage, stock or wine, and seasonings.
Cook on medium-high heat to reduce
the liquid and mingle the flavours. Add a
little tomato juice if the sauce seems too
thin. Toss with prepared noodles—try
rigatoni or rotini.

Cream Sauces

Always use whipping cream. The more you simmer the cream, the thicker the sauce will become. Despite concerns about high fat, cream sauces remain tremendously popular and are delicious and easy to prepare.

SERVES 4

Alfredo

1/2 cup whipping cream

1/4 cup parmesan (Parmigiano-Reggiano)

1/4 cup dry white wine

generous twists of black pepper

1/4 cup parsley, chopped

METHOD

Simmer all ingredients together until thickened. Toss with cooked fettuccine (the most traditional pasta for this sauce) and parsley to coat the noodles.

Lucinda's

2 green onions, chopped

1 Tbsp. olive oil

1/4 cup sun-dried tomatoes, chopped

1/4 cup softened goat cheese, crumbled

1/2 cup whipping cream

2 cups smoked turkey or chicken

METHOD

Sauté the green onions in olive oil. Add tomatoes, cheese, whipping cream, and chicken or turkey and simmer until thick. Toss with linguine or fettuccine and season with freshly ground pepper. Omit the chicken or turkey and it still tastes great.

Pesto Cream

Simmer 2 tablespoons of John's Basil Pesto (see page 116) with 1 cup whipping cream until thick. Toss with any pasta. Top with parmesan cheese.

Salmon Cream

2 salmon fillets, poached in water with some lemon, white wine, and dill

1/4 cup poaching liquid

3/4 cup cream

METHOD

Crumble salmon into a saucepan with the rest of the ingredients and simmer until thick. Toss with cooked pasta, such as large shells, rotini, or farfale.

SIDE DISHES & CONDIMENTS

A Plea to Non-Diners

SIDE DISHES

Steamed Green Vegetables

Stewed Red Cabbage

Roasted Root Vegetables

Pecorino Potatoes

Curried Sweet Potatoes

Biryani Rice

Rösti Potato Pancakes

Stir-Fry Rice Noodles

CONDIMENTS

John's Basil Pesto

Rhubarb Chutney

Apple Plum Chutney

Three-Pepper Relish

Coriander Chutney

Mushroom Salsa

Caponata

Salsa Fresca

Tropical Fruit Salsa

Cucumber Raita

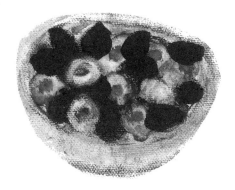

A Plea to Non-Diners

With The Bookshelf's new renovations recently completed, and a beautiful dining room and bar my new working environment, I hope to be spared the nightmare of trying to feed people who have something altogether different in mind. I'm not sure whether using restaurants as meeting places is a new phenomenon, or just a symptom of the last café incarnation's limitations, but I remember a night, not long ago, when I wondered whether continuing in the service industry was more than I could bear.

I was working alone in The Bookshelf's old dining room, the main food-service component of a unique business that also housed an exceptional bookstore, a small cinema, a second-story bar, and a rooftop terrace. The coming of the corporate bookstore invasion precipitated a renovation creating a small coffee shop as well as a dining room some have described as a nicely appointed hallway. On most nights, a single server with a bit of brain and hustle could handle the 14 tables. There were some evenings, however, when all hell broke loose and one could see the pity in the eyes of the customers as they watched the bald, middle-aged man (me) fly past their tables, sweat beading up on his reflecting dome, gamely trying to keep it all together.

To make matters worse, the kitchen was a football field away, at the very back of the bookstore. I will always resent the coming of Chapters for forcing The Bookshelf's owners, Barb and Doug Minett, to place the café and bistro at the front of the building. On busy nights, I could be heard saying "excuse me" countless times, rushing past readers as they quietly perused poetry books, furiously flipped through business tomes, or salivated over the latest culinary opus. Carrying four oversized plates full of steaming food while running a slalom course through spaced-out readers was hardly a picnic. There were times when I was forced to wonder whether this situation wasn't some kind of sick joke. Needless to say, this was no ordinary restaurant situation.

Back to the other night. Things were moving along very pleasantly. At approximately 7 p.m., about 65 percent of the room was filled with just the right number of tables having dessert, working on their dinners, or about to order. No problem! Returning to the bistro's narrow front entrance, having taken a drink order, I encountered three casually dressed women, teachers I guessed, who said they would be a party of five. "For dinner?" I automatically asked. They nodded, so I told them that it would take me a moment to set up a table and left them at the door.

Despite over 20 years in the business, I pride myself on maintaining an open mind where customer stereotypes are concerned. I do not assume that all parties of women will ask for separate checks, that the food won't be hot enough for certain older couples, or that teachers are always poor tippers. In fact, just about everyone is a poor tipper lately, unless it's another food-service worker. Therefore, when faced with the prospect of a group of women in sweats, carrying books and binders, I thought nothing of it.

I escorted the women through the noisy bistro to the back table (the best in the house), presented the menus, evening specials, and wine list and left them to await the arrival of the rest of their party. I had many other tables to tend to, a nice selection in fact, all enjoying the evening. When the others failed to arrive within five minutes, I approached the table and offered a drink before dinner. Two women ordered decaf, the other, regular coffee. Having been raised by a New Yorker who drank pots of coffee daily, I am never surprised when someone orders it before dinner, even though I favour a dry martini. A gullible sucker to the end, I was undeterred. Why else would I still be doing this job?

Finally, the last two women arrived. The first ordered a cappuccino and the other, obviously the group radical, a hot toddy. After waiting the requisite amount of time, I returned to the book-strewn table and politely asked what they would like for dinner. It was now 7:20, peak dining time, and I was turning away customers at the door.

"Oh, we aren't going to have anything to eat," offered the wild one, emboldened by the rum, "just these drinks while we have our little meeting." I was absolutely dumb-struck. I grabbed the menus off the table and frankly told them how rude I considered their behaviour. They didn't respond at all. Perhaps they had learned in teacher's college how to avoid confrontation by ignoring someone else's demands. I shudder at the thought that these women might pass on their lack of restaurant manners to a new generation of diners.

I glared at them for the rest of the evening. No more coffee was proffered as I would have felt compelled to charge them and, no matter how petty, considered billing for refills to be beneath me. Better to deny them. Finally, I presented the bill, which they ignored for over an hour, and, when shutting off the music failed to get their attention, I was forced to turn out the lights in order to get them to leave. I was inconsolable. The total bill came to $12.50, which of course, was all I found on the plate.

I have served people who have danced for joy on tables, slid off banquettes because they were so passionately entwined, wept openly because their lover chose our restaurant as the scene of a breakup, or writhed on the floor in a drunken frenzy while an entire dining room watched in appalled amazement. The one thing that all these patrons shared was their participation in the dining experience, however bizarre. What happened to the days when people invited others into their homes to work on projects and left the restaurant tables to those who wished to dine!? I wonder what is to become of poor restauranteurs and their unsuspecting army of servers if customers simply take up space.

SIDE DISHES

Steamed Green Vegetables

We have always valued the presence of a crisp, green vegetable as a side dish with any meal. Choose asparagus, beans, broccoli, or snap peas; each enlivens the plate and is a solid accompanist, no matter what the tune.

Using a steamer placed above boiling water, steam desired vegetable, covered, until cooked but still crisp. The vegetables will be a more brilliant green than before steaming. Serve with a wedge of lemon or a pat of butter or herbed butter.

Stewed Red Cabbage

SERVES 6

1 small red cabbage, sliced

1 cup chicken stock, water, or
   vegetable stock

splash of red wine vinegar

1/2 tsp. cumin

1/2 tsp. cinnamon

salt and pepper, to taste

METHOD

Place the sliced cabbage in a large pot with the stock or water. Add the vinegar and spices and simmer until the cabbage has softened, about 20 minutes. If all the liquid is absorbed and cabbage is still not soft, add more liquid to avoid burning.

Roasted Root Vegetables

SERVES 6

2 sweet potatoes, peeled and cut
  in wedges

3 potatoes, scrubbed and cut in wedges

1 small squash, peeled and cut in chunks

1 turnip, peeled and cut in chunks

1 large onion, cut in wedges

1 fennel bulb, sliced (optional)

splash olive oil

1 Tbsp. paprika

2 cloves garlic, minced or 1 tsp. garlic
  powder

salt and pepper, to taste

METHOD

Toss vegetables in a bowl and coat with
olive oil and spices. Pour into ovenproof
dish and bake at 375° F for about 1 hour,
turning once, until vegetables are soft on
the inside and crisp on the outside.

*Any combination of the suggested
vegetables will work with this recipe. If
you can think of a veggie we've forgotten,
then add it as well.*

Pecorino Potatoes

SERVES 4

1/3 cup pecorino or parmesan cheese,
   grated

1/3 cup breadcrumbs

1/4 cup Italian parsley, chopped

extra-virgin olive oil

4-5 medium potatoes, peeled and
   very thinly sliced

salt and ground pepper, to taste

METHOD

Preheat oven to 350° F. In a small bowl, mix together cheese, breadcrumbs, and chopped parsley. Coat the bottom of a pie plate or shallow baking dish with olive oil and completely cover with one layer of potatoes. Sprinkle with salt and pepper, cover with 1/3 of the cheese mixture and drizzle lightly with olive oil. Repeat to make three layers and top with the breadcrumb mixture. Bake for 30 to 45 minutes, until potatoes are soft and the top is crispy.

For an added treat, add one layer of thinly sliced artichoke hearts.

Curried Sweet Potatoes

SERVES 4

After mashed bananas, and before avocado, baked sweet potatoes, with a squeeze of fresh orange juice, were among the first foods we ever served our babies. As a result, we have a particular fondness for this most beautiful vegetable.

4 sweet potatoes, peeled and cut in
   2-inch chunks

2 Tbsp. unsalted butter

juice of 1 orange

1 Tbsp. curry powder

salt and pepper, to taste

METHOD

Place sweet potatoes in a large pot, cover with water, and boil for about 20 minutes, until tender. Drain potatoes and mash with butter, orange juice, curry powder, salt, and ground pepper.

Biryani Rice

SERVES 4

2 Tbsp. olive oil

1 cup basmati rice, rinsed and drained

1 Tbsp. ginger, grated

1 Tbsp. garlic, minced

1 Tbsp. garam masala, an Indian spice mixture (optional)

1 green onion, chopped

1 tsp. salt

2 1/2 cups water

1 Tbsp. sesame seeds, toasted

1 Tbsp. almonds or peanuts, toasted

1 Tbsp. currants

METHOD

In a large pot, heat olive oil and add rice, ginger, garlic, garam masala, and onions. Sauté the ingredients, stirring constantly. Add the salt, making sure the rice is coated. Add water, bring to a boil, and reduce the liquid until there is no excess water in the pot or cover with foil and bake for 15 to 20 minutes. Remove from oven and stir in sesame seeds, nuts, and currants.

Rösti Potato Pancakes

SERVES 4-6

4 large potatoes, peeled

1 small onion, grated

1 Tbsp. vegetable oil

salt and ground pepper, to taste

1 Tbsp. unsalted butter

METHOD

Boil potatoes in salted water until slightly softened, yet still firm. If overcooked, the starch will no longer work to hold the rosti together. Drain and set aside to cool. When cool enough to handle, coarsely grate the potato and the onion together in a bowl and season with plenty of salt and pepper. Form into thin patties. Using a non-stick frying pan on high heat, melt the butter with the oil and fry patties, pressing down with a spatula, until golden on both sides. Keep prepared rosti in a warm oven until ready to serve.

We serve these with breakfast egg dishes, but they are an excellent accompaniment to any dish. They also make a flat foundation for appetizers like Caponata (see page 121). For a variation, grate 1 sweet potato in with the regular potatoes.

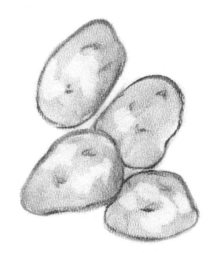

Stir-Fry Rice Noodles

This is an all-purpose, Asian-flavoured side dish. It is wonderful with salmon, chicken, or shrimp. Tossed with a variety of julienned vegetables, sprouts, and tofu, it becomes a great vegetarian main course.

FOR 4 SERVINGS

1 Tbsp. sesame oil

1 Tbsp. garlic, minced

1 Tbsp. ginger

1 package medium rice noodles, prepared as to package instructions

2 Tbsp. soy sauce

juice of 1 orange

1 Tbsp. orange rind, grated

hot sauce, to taste

2 green onions, chopped

a scant handful of fresh coriander leaves

METHOD

Heat sesame oil in a wok on high heat. Before it starts to smoke, add garlic and ginger. Quickly add prepared noodles, soy sauce, orange juice and rind, and hot sauce and toss for approximately 2 minutes. Add onions and coriander and continue tossing mixture for another minute. Noodles should be firm. Serve immediately.

When tossing the noodles, use long-handled tongs or two large spoons.

CONDIMENTS

John's Basil Pesto

John Medina has graced our kitchen for the past six years with kindness, hard work, and his magnificent baritone. A kitchen that hums with good energy and co-operation makes even the hardest days easier. I could always count on John to fix a leaky tap, come to the rescue in a crisis, or teach a new kid the ropes. Starting with a love of cooking, he learned the trade from the ground up, which he claims was necessary because his mother was such an awful cook. Among his many contributions is this recipe for pesto, a variation on the very popular condiment.

8 cloves garlic, crushed

**8 cups fresh basil, cleaned, chopped,
   tightly packed**

1/2 cup pine nuts, toasted

splash of olive oil

juice of 1 lemon

METHOD

In a food processor or blender, purée the garlic and basil. Scrape down the sides and add the pine nuts, lemon juice, and olive oil and process until smooth.

Pesto is great tossed with pasta and parmesan, added to tomato sauce or soup, spread on a pizza, or mixed with mayonnaise on a sandwich. It keeps for a long time and freezes well. The smell of fresh basil is heavenly.

Rhubarb Chutney

The first time I was ever in close proximity to rhubarb, actually growing in the ground, was in 1973, at a ramshackle homestead in the Ottawa Valley called Spring Green. Thirteen friends, for a variety of reasons, invested $18,500 to purchase a 186-acre piece of hardscrabble with a big albatross of a house, a muddy pond, and a rundown barnyard. There was no electricity or running water.

In the kitchen garden, growing as a companion plant to the twitch grass, was a big clump of goofy-looking rhubarb. I had no idea what to do with it as rhubarb was unheard of in my mother's kitchen. Luckily, our friend, Miriam Clavir, had a wonderful recipe for Branston Pickle that was the pride of her favourite aunt, Cammy. The original recipe called for 24 cups of rhubarb and 32 onions, so if you have a big patch and want to do some canning, then quadruple this recipe. This chutney is delicious with game hens, a complement to pork, and a great condiment with sliced meat and cheeses.

6 cups rhubarb, chopped

4 onions, chopped

1 1/2 cups brown sugar

1 1/2 cups cider vinegar

1 tsp. cinnamon

1 tsp. allspice

1/2 tsp. cayenne

1 tsp. salt

METHOD
Put all ingredients in a large saucepot, bring to a boil, reduce heat and simmer until thick and jam-like—about 1 hour. Cool and store in the refrigerator.

For a variation of this recipe, substitute about 2 1/2 cups of cranberries or chopped apples for the rhubarb.

Apple Plum Chutney

1 cup onions, chopped

2 1/2 cups apples, peeled and chopped

2 1/2 cups plums, chopped

rind of 2 oranges, pith removed, chopped

1/2 cup lemon juice

1 whole lemon, pitted and chopped
(peel and all)

1 1/2 cups white vinegar

1 cup firmly packed brown sugar

1 tsp. cinnamon

1 tsp. nutmeg

1 tsp. ground ginger

pinch of cayenne

drop of Tabasco sauce

METHOD

Place all ingredients in a large heavy saucepan and bring to a boil, stirring occasionally. Cook for approximately 1 hour, until thick and syrupy. Cool and store in the refrigerator.

This is a wonderful chutney for the fall. It is delicious as a complement to turkey and other fowl. Put the chutney in a jar, tie a ribbon around it, and you have a perfect gift.

Three-Pepper Relish

Relish, salsa, and chutney are the easiest way to add an exciting dimension to dishes. This relish is terrific as an omelet filling, as a lively accompaniment to any grilled meat or fish, and can even perk up prepared vegetarian burgers and hot-dogs.

3 sweet red peppers, seeded and diced

3 green peppers, seeded and diced

3 jalapeño peppers, seeded and diced

Place in heavy saucepan with:

1 cup brown sugar

1 1/2 cups cider vinegar

METHOD

Simmer, stirring occasionally, until liquid is reduced and the texture is syrupy, approximately 1/2 hour. Be careful not to let the relish burn. Cool and store in the refrigerator.

Coriander Chutney

This recipe is such a favourite that when the CBC held a condiment contest, we boldly entered. When it didn't win, we were crestfallen and licked our wounds by presuming that they either disqualified us as professionals or else hated coriander. Despite the fact that it has brought us no public glory, we still consider this recipe to be the most distinctly delicious condiment in our repertoire.

1 small onion, cut in quarters

2-3 jalapeño peppers, seeded

1 inch fresh ginger, peeled and chopped

2 cups fresh coriander, stems removed

1 green pepper, seeded and coarsely
  chopped

1 tsp. granulated sugar

1 tsp. salt

1/3 cup lemon juice

1/2 cup orange marmalade

METHOD

Using a food processor, chop onions, jalapeños, and ginger for 10 seconds. Add 1/2 of the coriander leaves and coarsely chop. Add remaining coriander, green pepper, sugar, and salt and purée. Add lemon juice and marmalade and continue processing until a paste forms. Cool and store in the refrigerator.

This recipe will yield more than you will need at one time. Save it for weeks in the refrigerator and it can be used to spice up any dish with lamb, goat cheese, or other strong-flavoured meats and cheeses.

Mushroom Salsa

Mushrooms are rarely the main ingredient in a salsa because they keep for such a short time. This is definitely not a problem with this creation, because it is so excellent that there will be none left at the end of the meal.

3 cups diced mushrooms, a combination
   is best
3 Tbsp. olive oil
1 tsp. coarse salt
1 tsp. ground pepper
1 tsp. cumin
3 Tbsp. jalapeño peppers, seeded and
   finely chopped
2 green onions, chopped
1/4 cup fresh coriander, chopped
3 Tbsp. lime juice

METHOD
Sauté mushrooms in the oil for approximately 2 minutes. Transfer to a bowl and let cool. Add the remaining ingredients and combine well. Use immediately, or store briefly, covered, in the refrigerator.

Caponata

1 medium eggplant

salt

2 Tbsp. extra-virgin olive oil

1 small onion, diced

2 stalks celery, diced

1 red pepper, seeded and diced

1 green pepper, seeded and diced

1/4 cup capers

1/4 cup green olives, sliced

generous splash of red wine vinegar

4 ripe tomatoes, diced or 1/4 cup tomato
  sauce

salt and ground pepper, to taste

handful of pine nuts, toasted

METHOD

To prepare eggplant, dice it (1/4- to 1/2-inch cubes) with the peel on, then let it sit, salted, for 1/2 hour. Rinse and pat dry. In a large pan, sauté eggplant in the olive oil, stirring until soft and browned. Remove from pan and set aside. In the same pan, with a little more oil, sauté onions, celery, and peppers for about 5 minutes. Return the eggplant, then add capers, olives, vinegar, and tomatoes and let stew 5 minutes more. Season with salt and pepper and lastly, add pine nuts. Cook briefly and remove from pan. Store covered in a bowl in the refrigerator.

This versatile relish is wonderful as a topping for bruschetta, as a condiment with baked fish or burgers, or even tossed with pasta. It can be served hot or at room temperature, and is great as a pizza topping, an omelet filling, or on top of crackers as hors d'oeuvres.

Salsa Fresca

8 fresh tomatoes, seeded and diced

2 fresh or pickled jalapeño peppers,
    seeded and diced

1/2 onion, finely chopped

2 cloves garlic, minced

1 cup coriander leaves, chopped

1/2 sweet red pepper, seeded and diced

1/2 green pepper, seeded and diced

2 Tbsp. parsley, chopped

2 Tbsp. olive oil

juice of 1 lime

1 tsp. ground coriander

3 tsp. ground cumin

pinch of salt

pinch of granulated sugar

METHOD

Drain diced tomatoes in a colander, then combine with remaining ingredients. Allow to sit for about an hour before serving. This salsa has a brief shelf life.

Salsa Fresca variations: Add chopped avocado just before serving; substitute roasted red pepper for fresh; use fresh basil or oregano instead of coriander and cumin; add chopped green olives.

Tropical Fruit Salsa

1/2 red onion, finely chopped

1 mango, diced

1/2 cantaloupe, diced

2 fresh jalapeños, seeded and diced

1/4 cup coriander leaves, finely chopped

the juice of 2 limes

splash of olive oil

2 oranges, sectioned and chopped, pith
removed

1 grapefruit, sectioned and chopped, pith
removed

METHOD

Combine all ingredients in a bowl, cover
and chill for at least 1 hour.

*This salsa is a wonderful complement to
grilled fish, chicken, or any Mexican
meal.*

Cucumber Raita

In our vegetarian years, we lived with a friend named Gene Freott. Whenever we made a delicious curry feast, Geno would prepare a cucumber raita to cool our burning palates.

Much like our Cocker Spaniel, Piper, our two young daughters, Kael and Terra, were constantly underfoot when anyone was working in the kitchen. Geno always had the patience to answer their questions or put Terra, the one who truly loved food, up on the counter beside him.

"What are you making Geno?" Terra asked in her throaty, pre-adenoid-removal voice.

"I'm making a 'Lefta!'" answered Gene with a sly grin.

"No! No! No! It's a raita, not a lefta!" giggled Terra, who adored the silliness.

I just spoke to Terra on the phone, and she tried to take credit for making the joke to begin with. Precocious she was, but our beloved Geno made the dish and dubbed it "Lefta."

2 cups plain yogourt

1/2 English cucumber, diced

2 green onions, finely chopped

1/2 tsp. fresh mint, chopped

1 tsp. fresh coriander, chopped

pinch of cayenne

pinch of cumin

salt and ground pepper, to taste

METHOD

Stir all ingredients together and chill.

DESSERTS

Two Tarts

Belgian Chocolate Paté

Pecan Chocolate Pie

Glenna's Apple Crisp

Niagara Peach Torte

Bookshelf Fruit Crisp with Pastry Bottom

Warm Pecan Brownie

White Chocolate Raspberry Mousse

Almond Meringues

Fruit Compote

Lemon Cream Pie

Nutty Fudge and Cream Cheese Pie

Bookshelf Carrot Cake with
   Cream Cheese Icing

Crème Anglaise

Caramel Sauce

Fabulous Chocolate Sauce

Most-Trusted Pie Pastry

Two Tarts

Bronwyn Pritchard, a doe-eyed waif of a girl with a will of steel, was the first real pastry chef that we ever worked with. Fresh from a stint at a classy Vancouver hotel, she had returned to Ottawa with her husband and wished to re-establish the reputation for excellence she had earned at the defunct Black Cat Café.

Having kept abreast of the restaurant scene in Ottawa, Bronwyn was aware that Grenville's was the critical darling of the moment and she wrote us a timely letter of introduction. We snapped her up, as we were managing the desserts ourselves and certainly needed some help.

Over the next year, Bronwyn wowed us, the public, and critics alike with her repertoire of incredible delights. Like a roller-derby star, she elbowed the big kitchen boys out of the way and made her presence felt in everything she did. Sadly for us, she retired from the rough life of a pastry chef when she became pregnant with her and John's first child.

One of the greatest benefits of Bronwyn's tenure was the skill she passed on to our partner, Chris Grenville. A mutual admiration was immediately established between these two lovely women, and Chris, one of Ottawa's premier bakers to this day, carried the baton Bronwyn gladly passed to her. In the years since leaving Ottawa, we have begged, borrowed, and stolen ideas and recipes from these two sterling talents. They have our humble thanks and admiration.

Belgian Chocolate Paté

This is a flourless cake that is rich, delicious, and serves as many as 16 people. It keeps for a week if refrigerated.

16 oz. Belgian chocolate, chopped

1/2 lb. unsalted butter

6 eggs, at room temperature

1/2 cup Fabulous Chocolate Sauce

   (see page 141)

crème Anglaise (optional) (see page 139)

METHOD

Preheat oven to 425° F. Prepare a 10-inch springform pan by cutting a circle of waxed or parchment paper, layering the bottom, and buttering the entire inside of the pan, including the paper. Wrap the outside of the pan in aluminum foil.

Melt the chocolate with the butter in a stainless steel bowl set atop a pot of boiling water (or use a double boiler) and set aside. Whisk the eggs in another stainless steel bowl over the heat until they are warm, then transfer to an electric mixer on low speed. Gradually increase the speed and whip until pale, light, puffy, and greatly increased in volume. The eggs should triple in volume.

Add 1/2 of the egg mixture to the melted chocolate and mix well, then fold in the remaining eggs until streaks disappear. Pour 1/2 of the mixture into the prepared pan and drizzle with 1/2 cup Fabulous Chocolate Sauce on top. Carefully add the remaining mixture, spread evenly, and drizzle top decoratively with the rest of the chocolate sauce.

Set springform pan in a larger baking pan filled partially with water (a water bath) and bake at 425° F for 5 minutes. Cover with foil and bake for 10 minutes more. Lift from water bath, remove all the foil, and place on a rack to cool. The paté will not be completely set. Chill for at least 3 hours before removing from pan and serving.

To unmold, take a hot towel and wrap it around the springform ring to loosen and remove. Put the ring back on. Turn the torte upside down on a board and place the hot towel on the bottom until the cake slides away from the pan. Remove the parchment from the bottom, invert the pan onto a serving tray and remove the ring.

Slice and serve on a pool of crème Anglaise and top with more chocolate sauce.

Pecan Chocolate Pie

For one prepared pie crust, use store-bought or our Most-Trusted Pie Pastry (see page 142).

1 2/3 cups corn syrup

1 1/4 cups brown sugar

2/3 cup unsalted butter

5 eggs

2 tsp. vanilla

1/2 cup pecans, chopped

1/4 cup pecans, whole

handful of semi-sweet chocolate chips or
    cut-up chocolate

METHOD

In a medium saucepan, cook the corn syrup, brown sugar, and butter on low heat until the sugar is dissolved. Remove from heat.

In a large bowl, beat the eggs with the vanilla and stir in the sugar mixture.

Cover the unbaked pie pastry with chopped pecans and sprinkle with chocolate chips or cut-up chocolate. Cover with filling, and then top with whole pecans and arrange attractively. Bake at 350° F for 40 to 45 minutes until firm. Cool and serve.

For an extra kick, add 1 oz. bourbon to the filling. For a tremendous treat, serve with Breyer's O'Henry Ice Cream, which is outstanding!

Glenna's Apple Crisp

SERVES 4-6

4-6 cups tart apples, peeled, cored, and
cut in chunks
juice of 1 lemon
1 tsp. cinnamon
1 Tbsp. granulated sugar

Toss all ingredients and place in lightly greased 8- x 12-inch baking pan.

Crumble together with your fingers until well mixed:

1/4 cup granulated sugar
1/4 cup brown sugar
1 1/2 cups rolled oats
1 tsp. cinnamon
1 Tbsp. flour
1/2 cup unsalted butter, cut in small pieces
1/4 cup almonds, pecans, or walnuts,
chopped

METHOD
Cover apples with crumble mixture and bake at 350° F for about an hour. Serve warm with ice cream, whipped cream, or sweetened yogourt.

This recipe is guaranteed to make any house smell absolutely great.

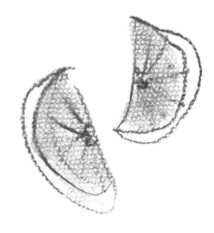

Niagara Peach Torte

SERVES 6-8

6 peaches, peeled and cut into wedges

1/3 cup granulated sugar

1/2 tsp. cinnamon

METHOD

Toss together in a bowl and set aside to form a syrup.

FOR THE BOTTOM PASTRY

1/2 cup unsalted butter

1/3 cup granulated sugar

1 cup all-purpose flour

METHOD

Pulse in a food processor or mix by hand until combined to form crumbly pastry. Press mixture into the bottom of a 10-inch springform pan and set aside. Preheat oven to 350° F.

FOR THE FILLING

8 oz. softened cream cheese

1 egg

1/2 tsp. vanilla

1 tsp. lemon juice

METHOD

Whip together or mix in a food processor until smooth. Pour filling over the pastry in the springform pan, and spread evenly. Place peaches decoratively to cover, and drizzle peaches with remaining syrup. Bake for 30 minutes and then sprinkle with:

1/4 cup sliced almonds

Bake for 10 minutes longer until filling is firm and almonds are toasted. Let cool, remove from springform pan, and slide onto cake plate. Serve cold.

This torte is delicious drizzled with Caramel Sauce (see page 140). We also make this recipe with apples and it is equally scrumptious.

Bookshelf Fruit Crisp with Pastry Bottom

SERVES 8

Line the bottom of an 8- x 12-inch baking pan with our Most-Trusted Pie Pastry (see page 142).

4-6 cups fresh or frozen fruit

1/4 cup granulated sugar

1/4 cup brown sugar

1 tsp. cinnamon

2-3 Tbsp. all-purpose flour

METHOD

Toss fresh or frozen fruit, anything from peaches to rhubarb to berries, alone or in combination, with the remaining ingredients. Cover pastry layer with fruit.

FOR THE TOPPING

1/4 cup granulated sugar

1/4 cup brown sugar

3/4 cup rolled oats

1/4 cup wheat germ, toasted briefly in oven or a dry frying pan

1/2 cup all-purpose flour

1/2 cup softened unsalted butter

pinch of salt

pinch of nutmeg

1/2 tsp. cinnamon

METHOD

Work together all ingredients with your fingers to form a crumble. Cover fruit and bake at 350° F for 45 minutes or until the top has browned. Serve warm with ice cream, whipped cream, or all by itself.

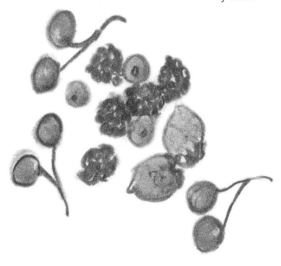

Warm Pecan Brownie

SERVES 8

1 1/2 cups unsalted butter

2 cups granulated sugar

2 tsp. vanilla

3/4 cup cocoa

4 eggs

2 cups all-purpose flour

2 Tbsp. baking powder

1/2 tsp. salt

1 cup pecans

1 cup semi-sweet chocolate chips

METHOD

With an electric mixer, cream the butter, sugar, and vanilla. Add the cocoa, and then the eggs, one at a time. Sift together the flour, baking powder, and salt and add to the mixer. Then blend in pecans and chocolate chips. Spread mixture into greased 8- x 12-inch baking pan. Bake at 350° F for 30 minutes.

For a dessert treat that brings back memories of childhood birthday parties, serve brownie warm with a big scoop of vanilla ice cream and Caramel Sauce (see page 140). Decadent and delicious!

White Chocolate Raspberry Mousse

SERVES 4-6

2 cups raspberries

1/8 cup cassis

4 egg whites

1 Tbsp. granulated sugar

1/4 tsp. cream of tartar

1 cup whipping cream

6 oz. white chocolate, chopped

3/4 cup milk

1 Tbsp. gelatin

1/2 cup cold water

METHOD

Purée the raspberries with the cassis in a food processor or blender. (If using frozen raspberries, thaw before blending.) Beat the egg whites with the sugar and cream of tartar until stiff enough to form peaks. Set aside. In a separate bowl, whip the cream until it almost forms peaks. Set aside. Melt the chocolate with the milk over a double boiler and transfer to a large bowl. In a small pan, sprinkle gelatin over water and gently heat to dissolve, and then stir the gelatin and the berries into the chocolate. Gently fold in the egg whites and then the whipped cream. Pour into individual dessert goblets or a serving bowl and refrigerate until set.

We make another dessert using this mousse, which incorporates chocolate angel food cake. Simply crumble slices of cake and layer it with the mousse in a bowl or in individual serving glasses, like a trifle. The combination of chocolate cake with the raspberry mousse is outstanding.

Almond Meringues

3/4 cup almonds

1/2 cup plus 8 tsp. granulated or
  extra-fine sugar

1 Tbsp. cornstarch

4 egg whites at room temperature

1/8 tsp. cream of tartar

METHOD

Finely grind the nuts with 1/2 cup sugar in a food processor. Transfer to a medium bowl and sift the cornstarch on top. Stir with a fork to blend.

Using an electric mixer on medium speed, blend the egg whites with the cream of tartar until soft peaks are formed. Increase the speed to high and gradually add the remaining 8 teaspoons of sugar. Beat until stiff and shiny but not dry.

Sprinkle 1/3 of the nut mixture over the beaten egg whites and gently fold in by hand, until just combined. Repeat with the remaining nut mixture.

Line 2 cookie sheets with parchment paper and draw 6 3-inch circles on each. Using a spoon, place individual mounds of meringue onto the drawn circles and spread to 1/2-inch thickness. Bake at 300° F for 30 minutes, and then reduce heat to 275° F and bake for another 10 minutes. Remove from parchment for cooling. Serve with Fruit Compote (see page 135), ice cream, Raspberry Mousse (see page 133), lemon mousse, or berries and whipped cream.

Fruit Compote

SERVES 6

3 cups water

1/2 cup granulated sugar

3 strips lemon zest (peel without the
   white pith)

1/4 cup red wine

3 tart apples, peeled, cored, and sliced

1 cinnamon stick or 6 whole allspice berries

3 firm pears, peeled, cored, and sliced

12 prunes, pitted

METHOD

Bring the water, sugar, lemon zest, red
wine, and cinnamon stick or allspice to a
boil in a non-aluminum saucepan. Boil
for 5 minutes, reduce the heat, and drop
in the apples. Simmer for 10 minutes and
then add the pears, poach for 5 minutes,
add the prunes, and cook for 2 minutes
longer. Remove from heat and cool.

Serve fruit with some poaching liquid
in a bowl.

*If you wish, you may add berries or
pomegranate seeds before serving.
Excellent with Almond Meringues (see
page 134). Great with ice cream or
yogourt crème Chantilly, which is made
by whisking plain yogourt with a splash
of maple syrup or other sweetener.*

Lemon Cream Pie

Thomas King, the noted Canadian writer and educator, lives in Guelph and loves this dessert. We have always served it with blueberry sauce, which Tom does not like. He doesn't like ice with his water or caffeine in his coffee, or onions on his veggie burger either. We like Tom tremendously, and are happy to serve him whatever he likes, however he likes it!

SERVES 6

2 whole eggs

3 egg yolks

6 Tbsp. granulated sugar

2 lemons, grated and juiced

6 Tbsp. unsalted butter, cut in pieces

1 Most-Trusted Pie Pastry, pre-baked

   (see page 142)

METHOD

In a saucepan, over medium heat, stir eggs, egg yolks, and sugar together. Stir in lemon juice and peel along with the butter and then cook entire mixture, stirring constantly, until thickened enough to coat a wooden spoon. Remove from heat and let stand to thicken further. Whisk to remove any lumpy bits and fill prepared pie crust. Bake at 350° F for 10 to 15 minutes until set. Cool on a rack and then chill before serving. Top with sweetened whipped cream and/or berries.

   At our restaurants we garnish Lemon Cream Pie with blueberry sauce made by heating 2 cups blueberries (fresh or frozen) with the juice of 1 lemon, and 3 tablespoons of sugar. Mix 1 tablespoon cornstarch with 1/2 cup water and stir into the heating blueberries to thicken. Makes enough for 1 pie.

To pre-bake a pie crust, line the crust with foil and cover with dried beans or rice. The beans keep the crust from buckling. Bake for about 10 minutes at 350° F.

Nutty Fudge and
Cream Cheese Pie

SERVES 6-8

FOR THE PASTRY

2 cups all-purpose flour

1/2 cup sugar

1 cup unsalted butter, cut in pieces

METHOD

In a food processor, pulse ingredients to form a dough. Line a 10-inch springform pan by pressing the dough in with your fingers to cover the bottom and sides of the pan. Set aside.

FOR THE FUDGE

4 oz. semi-sweet chocolate, chopped

1/2 cup unsalted butter, cut in pieces

2 eggs

3/4 cup granulated sugar

1 Tbsp. flour

METHOD

Melt the chocolate and butter in a double boiler or stainless steel bowl set on top of a steaming pot of water. Meanwhile, whisk the eggs with the sugar. Add the melted chocolate mixture and the flour and continue whisking vigorously. Spread the fudge over the pastry and refrigerate until chocolate is hard.

FOR THE CHEESE

16 oz. cream cheese

1/2 cup granulated sugar

1 cup sour cream

1 tsp. vanilla

3 eggs

METHOD

In a food processor, mix the cream cheese with the sugar. Add the sour cream, vanilla, and the eggs and continue processing until smooth. Pour the cream cheese mixture on top of the hard chocolate and bake at 350° F for 30 minutes until the centre is set and firm. Let cool, remove from pan, cut in wedges, and garnish with Fabulous Chocolate Sauce (see page 141), Caramel Sauce (see page 140), and chopped unsalted pecans or peanuts.

Bookshelf Carrot Cake with Cream Cheese Icing

SERVES 10

2 cups carrots, grated

1 1/2 cups all-purpose flour

1 1/2 cups granulated sugar

1/2 tsp. salt

1/2 tsp. baking soda

2 tsp. cinnamon

3/4 cup vegetable oil

2 eggs, beaten

2 tsp. vanilla

3/4 cup pecans, chopped

3/4 cup unsweetened coconut

1 cup chopped pineapple, drained

METHOD

Cook the carrots quickly, about 7 minutes, in enough water to cover. Drain and set aside. Sift the dry ingredients into the large bowl of an electric mixer. Add the oil, eggs, and vanilla and beat well. Fold in the nuts, coconut, cooked carrots, and pineapple. Pour into a greased 10-inch springform pan and bake for 50 minutes at 350° F until a knife inserted into the centre comes out clean.

FOR THE ICING

8 oz. softened cream cheese

6 Tbsp. unsalted butter

3 cups icing sugar, sifted

1 tsp. vanilla

juice of 1/2 lemon

METHOD

Cream cheese and butter together in an electric mixer. With the mixer still beating, add the sugar and stir in vanilla and lemon juice until the mixture is smooth. When the cake has cooled to room temperature, cover with icing and sprinkle with toasted coconut. (Toast coconut in a toaster oven for about 10 minutes or in a pan in the oven alongside the cake. When it is aromatic and brown, it is done.)

Crème Anglaise

What can I say about crème Anglaise?
It's English cream, pronounced in French.
It's milky, beige, and not particularly
attractive, but it tastes wonderful and can
be dressed up in many ways.

1 cup whipping cream

1 cup milk

2 egg yolks

1/4 cup granulated sugar

METHOD

Heat the whipping cream and milk together in a saucepan to just below the boiling point. Do not boil. Remove from heat. In a bowl, beat the egg yolks with the sugar until smooth and thick. Combine half the hot cream mixture with the eggs, stir, and pour back into the saucepan so that the eggs don't curdle. Place on low heat, stirring constantly with a wooden spoon until mixture coats the spoon and is a nice consistency, like thin custard. Do not boil! Remove from heat and transfer to another container and chill. Stir again before serving.

Flavour with a splash of your favourite liqueur. If serving with Belgian Chocolate Paté (see page 127), try adding Cointreau and some orange zest or Kahlua with espresso beans to the crème Anglaise.

Caramel Sauce

1/2 cup corn syrup

2 cups granulated sugar

1 cup whipping cream

This recipe will yield quite a lot, but can be kept in the refrigerator for a long time. Heat it as you need it. Makes a terrific gift.

METHOD

Coat the bottom of a heavy frying pan with corn syrup and add sugar. Do not stir! Place on low heat, watch carefully, and once again, do not stir! Every so often, using a hot-pad, take the handle and shake the pan, so that the sugar melts evenly.

Once all the sugar is melted, turn heat to high, continue shaking occasionally, and watch for the colour to start changing under the bubbles.

When the sugar turns a "caramel" colour, remove from the heat and slowly stir in whipping cream using a wooden spoon, until bubbling has stopped.

Be careful not to allow sugar to get too dark as it will burn. Use only a wooden spoon, don't forget the oven mitts, and stir gently, trying not to splash. Nag! Nag! Nag!

Fabulous Chocolate Sauce

Warm chocolate sauce is heated on a mini hotplate all day long in restaurants. Our sauce is warm, runny, and smooth and makes a lovely ribbon of chocolate when drizzled over the dessert and plates. It makes everything taste better, especially if you're a person who loves chocolate.

6 oz. Belgian chocolate

4 Tbsp. cocoa

1/4 cup strong coffee

juice of 1 orange

1/3 cup water

3 Tbsp. unsalted butter

4 Tbsp. corn syrup

1/4 cup granulated sugar

METHOD

In a saucepan on low heat, melt the chocolate, cocoa, and coffee with the orange juice and water, stirring constantly with a wooden spoon. Remove from heat and add butter, corn syrup, and sugar. Return to low heat and continue stirring until smooth and thick enough to coat the spoon and "ribbon" back into the pan.

At home, you can heat the chocolate sauce in a makeshift double boiler, or a real one if you have it. Or, you can put the sauce in the microwave and heat if for about 30 seconds. Be careful, good chocolate burns easily.

Chocolate sauce keeps for a long time, covered in the refrigerator. Heat it as you need it.

Most-Trusted Pie Pastry

MAKES 6 9-INCH CRUSTS

It might seem excessive to make six pastries at once, but these freeze well and can be thawed and used whenever a pie crust is called for, both sweet and savoury.

6 cups pastry flour

1 tsp. salt

1 tsp. baking powder

1 Tbsp. brown sugar

1 lb. vegetable shortening

1 egg

1 Tbsp. white vinegar

ice water

METHOD

In a large bowl place flour, salt, baking powder, brown sugar, and shortening. Work ingredients together with a pastry cutter or two knives, until the mixture resembles coarse meal. Beat the egg with the vinegar. Add enough water to the egg and vinegar mixture to make 1 cup together. Quickly add to the flour, knead briefly, and form into 6 balls. Wrap them individually in wax paper or plastic wrap and chill.

Still Standing

It is the middle of April, and the snow refuses to stop falling. The emerging bulbs that hold spring's promise stand in a state of shock. Though my heart longs to be in the garden, the huge job of running the new Bookshelf Café is keeping me inside. A loather of winter, I am nevertheless thankful for the cold, as it soothes my gardener's spring lust and keeps the 50 extra dining seats that await on the lovely new courtyard under wraps.

No matter how hard one tries to prepare for the realities of a new restaurant, there is little to do but survive it. Unlike most new establishments that must find a clientele, The Bookshelf has been an institution for over 20 years and the renovations' nine-month gestation period has made the public very hungry for a taste of the new. We opened the doors and were swamped. Everyone wanted a piece of the action, and the effect on the staff, and on Glenna and me in particular, was something akin to being run over by a Buick.

It's not that I haven't been through this before. Six restaurant openings under my belt have helped me prepare psychologically for the onslaught of work that accompanies launching a venture such as this. I even exercised a serious amount of willpower and successfully lost a bit of weight—my way of getting into some sort of physical shape for what lay ahead. It had dawned on me, as the renovation began to evolve and the brilliant collaboration between the designer Martha Johnson and the builder Doug Minett became a reality, that The Bookshelf's rebirth might actually kill me! I am 51 years old, somewhat self-indulgent, not particularly physical, with a tendency toward high blood pressure. Each time one ventures back into the ring, so to speak, for another championship bout, it's always a question whether one will be still standing when the match is over.

The new restaurant is more than twice the size of its predecessor. It is very beautiful, with 14-foot ceilings, walls of glass at both ends, espresso suede horseshoe-shaped booths, a long, black bar, and restored hardwood floors. The walls of the back dining room have a stunning mural that was painted by the talented Ms Johnson, and the overall effect is both urban and warm. The people of Guelph are understandably thrilled to have such an exceptional new environment, and they have been clamouring to get in and get fed since day one.

About three days after the opening—three days of intense, gruelling work—we were standing in the parking lot after an endless lunch. Glenna burst into tears and informed me that she couldn't go on, that she was through. I can probably count on one hand, maybe two, the number of times Glenna has broken down emotionally over the past 30 years, so I knew that this was no idle threat. That said, I also knew that she only partially meant it and that if we put our heads together and gave it the old team try, we would survive. I also told her that she couldn't quit, period. She quickly got herself together, apologized for dumping on me, got into the car, and drove home for a nap. Thank God for naps!

If I sound a little overdramatic, let me say that I have worked a total of 357 hours over the past four weeks, without so much as a day off. Some days I go from waiting tables right into the kitchen without a break. On a directive from the owners, we hired no new staff to launch the new space and so all the extra work fell on us. When you're working 15 hours a day, handling all the issues, problems, and quirks that arise is no easy task, so the work just keeps piling up. Luckily, we have some great staff. Ann Molnar, a young woman who has worked for us for the past seven years, with a tenacity and spirit second to none, has been a lifesaver. The kitchen staff has responded to the challenge with amazing resilience and, with the exception of the occasional screamer, everyone here has been exceptional. We are slowly adding staff now—hosts and bus people, an extra baker here, a line cook there, and little by little things will calm down.

In the restaurant biz I feel a little like Cher—one more comeback under my belt. It's a wonderful feeling to have space to work in and a captive and receptive audience to play to. It's nice to dress up a little when working the floor, not only because I've lost 25 pounds, but also because the room is so lovely and gracious. Yesterday a grumpy-looking couple was standing by the entrance and, when I approached to ask if they would like a table for lunch, the women curtly asked to see a menu. "We were here the first day and it took 45 minutes for the meal to come," sneered the reptilian man. "You'd better be fast today!" "It was the first day," I politely responded. "And by the way, I don't have a table available." I removed the menu from his hand and left them standing there. How sweet it is!

Menu Terms

Chiffonade   Three or more leaves of lettuce, basil, etc. stacked on a flat surface, rolled into a tight cigar and cut into thin strips with a sharp knife. A lovely bed for quesadillas or a chicken salad.

Deglaze   To remove the brown bits that stick to the bottom of a pan when sautéing meat, fish, seafood, or vegetables in fat, by adding a splash of wine, stock, or other liquid. Deglazing enriches the flavour and improves the texture of the resulting sauce.

Emulsify   Combining oil or fat with an acid such as lemon or vinegar, whether with a whisk, blender, or food processor to make mayonnaise, mustards, and salad dressings. While rapidly beating the acid, slowly drizzle in the other.

Julienne   To uniformly cut vegetables into short thin matchsticks.

Purée   To finely blend or mash food until it is completely smooth.

Reduce   To make a reduction, bubble liquids such as stock, vinegar, wine, or whipping cream on high heat to reduce in volume and thicken. This intensifies flavour.

Sauté   To cook in a small amount of hot oil over high heat in an open pan. When oil is hot, add the ingredients and toss or stir with a wooden spoon. Sautéing releases flavour.

Spring Mix   A popular mix of tender young salad greens, washed and ready for use. A delicious timesaver.

Sweat   To cook vegetables in a small amount of liquid, such as water, vinegar, or oil, in a covered pot. This technique softens without browning, allowing the vegetables to cook in their own juices.

Index